the making of an activist

by Lekha Singh, Craig and Marc Kielburger

Christmas, 2009

Dear Klaire,

If this isn't (you), I don't know what is.

We love watching your life unfold!!

Love you,

Mom + Mike
xx   xx

Credits

Designed, compiled and edited by Lekha Singh, Craig Kielburger and Marc Kielburger.

All artwork, documents and photographs courtesy of Free The Children, except where noted.

Photographs by Lekha Singh: vii, 4-5, 8-9, 14, 16, 18-19 (background), 20 (background), 27, 47, 65, 135-136, 142-143, 173, 178, 185, 191, 194.

Design by Colin Drumm: 31, 34, 106-107.

Graphic art by Jack Swart: 32-33, 136, 168-169.

Hand lettering, collage and painting by Ryan LaMountain: vi, 54, 64-65, 82-83, 93, 118, 128-129, 133, 148-149, 198.

Photographs by Lloyd Hanoman: 31, 48, 83, 84, 137, 138, 189, 196, 197, 198, 199.

Photograph by Helaina Roman: 64.

Photograph by Ed Ou: 195.

Graphic artwork from Me to We by Craig Kielburger and Marc Kielburger courtesy of John Wiley & Sons: 74-75.

Graphic design courtesy of Adam Saltsman: 100-101.

Textile images from African Textiles by John Gillow courtesy of Chronicle Books: 2 (photo of radial textile, Longevity Studio, London); 58, 60 (photo, James Austin).

News clippings courtesy of the Toronto Star: 10, 91, 146.

Graphics courtesy of United Nations and UNICEF: 68- 69.

Publication cover art courtesy of the International Labour Office: 55.

News clipping courtesy of the Chicago Tribune: 70.

News clipping courtesy of the Telegram-Tribune: 71.

Table of Contents

This book starts when Lekha writes an **Introduction** vi

then, the *Activism starts* with The Spark 2

next thing is what to do now that you're sparked: The Work 56

you start to think, what's the world going to be like in The Future 164

That's when Craig and Marc write an **Afterword** 205

...and then thank a lot of awesome people in the **Acknowledgments** 213

Introduction

My most recent spark has been the children of Africa. While we can get started with a single spark, we must keep ourselves going by getting inspired every day.

This book offers you many sparks, ideas and examples. I hope it inspires you to put your energy into that which is meaningful to you and that which can truly change what is wrong in this world.

I would like to first thank Craig Kielburger and Marc Kielburger for being the inspiration for this book. I would also like to thank the children around the world, of all ages, who have contributed to this book and who are lighting our way into the future—including Eva Haller, Roxanne Joyal, Cheryl Perera, Ed Gillis, Nadja Halilbegovic, Anitra Sumbry, Dianna Hunter English, Jason Apostol, Sheena Kamal and Janet Cho.

A special thank you to Colin Drumm, Jack Swart, Ryan LaMountain and Joanna Zeller who made these pages sparkle and for long hours of putting the pages together.

With much love,
Lekha Singh

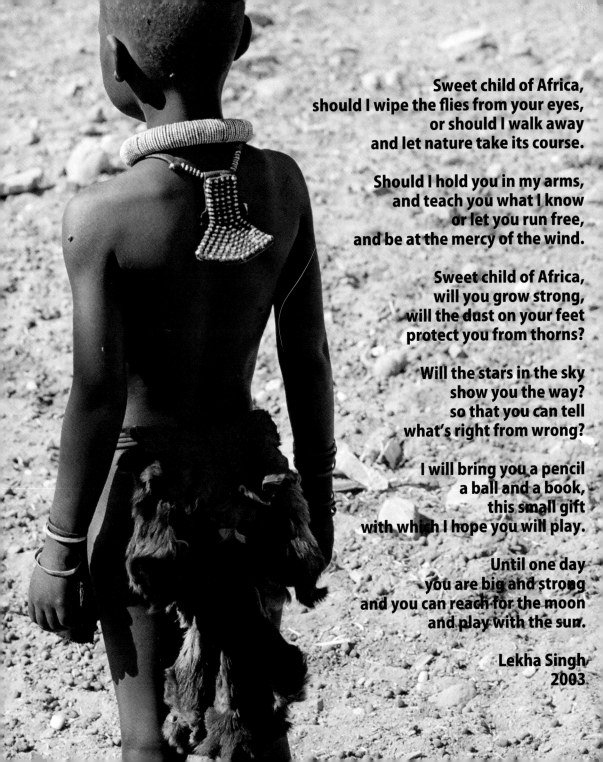

Sweet child of Africa,
should I wipe the flies from your eyes,
or should I walk away
and let nature take its course.

Should I hold you in my arms,
and teach you what I know
or let you run free,
and be at the mercy of the wind.

Sweet child of Africa,
will you grow strong,
will the dust on your feet
protect you from thorns?

Will the stars in the sky
show you the way?
so that you can tell
what's right from wrong?

I will bring you a pencil
a ball and a book,
this small gift
with which I hope you will play.

Until one day
you are big and strong
and you can reach for the moon
and play with the sun.

Lekha Singh
2003

rk

the spark

THE SPARK

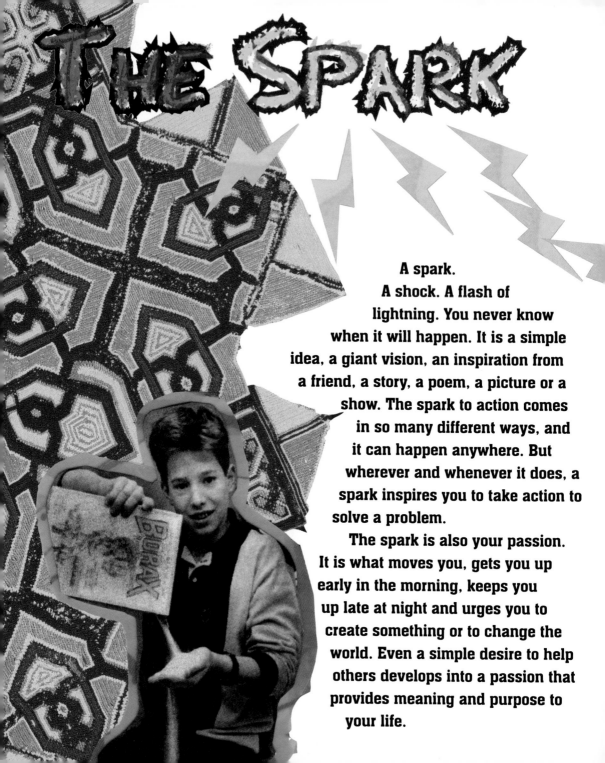

A spark.
A shock. A flash of
lightning. You never know
when it will happen. It is a simple
idea, a giant vision, an inspiration from
a friend, a story, a poem, a picture or a
show. The spark to action comes
in so many different ways, and
it can happen anywhere. But
wherever and whenever it does, a
spark inspires you to take action to
solve a problem.

The spark is also your passion.
It is what moves you, gets you up
early in the morning, keeps you
up late at night and urges you to
create something or to change the
world. Even a simple desire to help
others develops into a passion that
provides meaning and purpose to
your life.

You can make a difference no matter how young you are. Don't wait till you're grown up. Do it now. The pages in this book feature projects done by kids like you to change the lives of other kids in distant countries. Whether you raise money for building schools, collect items to send to kids who need them or take a trip to another country on a project to build a school, you can make a real difference.

The sparks in this book show what is possible when you think outside the box. An entire generation of kids has now grown up in Free The Children, and their stories and pictures will spark you, the next generation, to take action for a better world.

But that spark is just the beginning. Next, take the leap of faith, plan, do the work, join an organization or find support that encourages your activism in the community.

Some kids know early on exactly what their spark is. Most of us know that we have to get involved, but we don't know how. That's why it is important to define your spark, and to help your friends find their spark, so that you can make good choices in turning your passion into action.

PARAMESWARI FIREWORKS, SIVAK ISI.

We All Have Our Sparks   *by Craig Kielburger*

We all have our sparks—those moments of insight that ignite the passions of a lifetime. Some are large, others small. Some occur abroad, some appear closer to home. Sometimes they make us smile, often they move us to tears. Whatever the case, these sparks illuminate our lives, revealing paths we might otherwise not recognize as our own. These sparks are what make it possible to change the world.

Our sparks are as unique as each of us. My own passion for children's rights was first ignited by a headline in the morning paper, now forever engraved in my memory. That headline read: "Battled child labor, boy, 12, murdered." Just 12 years old myself, I could hardly believe that a boy my own age could be killed for standing up for the rights of children. I knew I had to do something.

When my brother Marc talks about his spark, he laughingly recalls how cleaning the house first launched him on the road to activism. Shocked by the hazard symbols on commercial cleaning products, Marc created a science fair project on environmentally friendly alternatives and went on to become a spokesperson for the environmental movement. Later, long months of service work in Asia and Africa convinced him of the need to end poverty and exploitation.

Sparks come in all shapes and sizes. Roxanne's arrived in the form of a young girl named Nan, stricken with AIDS. Eva's found fuel in the courage with which her older brother John defied the Nazis. Jason's passion for social justice work was set ablaze by a very special group of friends.

Whenever and wherever they occur, our sparks are things of beauty. They are incredibly powerful. Every time we discover one, we must let it burn bright!

I think child Labor is horrible!
I want to fight for childrens
rights! Children should be able
to have fun and play and go
on adventures when their still
young. It's not fair! please write
back as soon as possible
for more information for me.

Sincerly,
Nyrie Mckenzie
Nyrie Mc kenzia
10 years old
Albany N.Y

P.S. I support your effort on
fighting for children.

El salvador and many areas
like that. I wish I could do
something like show people so
me of the terrible happening
going on in the world. Many
people turn there backs as
if child labour was nothing!
I used to be like that. until
I saw the article's onTV and
in magazines about what you
did. one can't but if the work
got toghether, we could make
a difference.

please write back

Sarah
Murde
ch

7

When I Returned to San Francisco from Africa

Well, after chipping the dirt off my body, all I can feel is: I want to go back, right now, just drop everything and go! Although I came to the program the least experienced, I now feel I am the most changed. Along with Africa, you three have changed my life. Before I was this shy teenager who often took part in community service, but never exactly knew what really drove me in life. Although I still don't know my life plan (although I don't believe anyone does) I know from now on I am going to help people out as much as I can. I might not start my own organization, but I will do whatever I can to help the lives of those who need some loving care.

- Allison Sander

IN INDIA

India left its traces
in the form of
mosquito bites,
baggage bruises,
and dirt still lodged
under my finger nails,
but mosquito bites,
bruises,
and dirty finger nails
are not permanent,
the changes however,
that occurred
in my heart and mind
while pondering paradoxes
aboard 2nd class sleeper trains
at 3 in the morning
will be with me even after
I lay my head on an earthen pillow
and sleep forever…

…it is only now
Through the eyes
of a child
That I realize
What I have.
She with only her hands
Grabbed my soul
And pulled it forcefully
But kindly
and made me see
what I must be,
and now am…

…I look up and wait,
wait for something,
someone to come change
all of this.
As I stare into the
Indian sky after the
monsoon rain
I realize all I will ever see
Is endless blue
So I look down
And see humanity,
I see me.

- Lorissa Rinehart

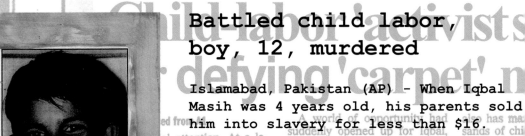

Iqbal Masih
Born 1982
Murdered 1995

Iqbal Masih, activist, murdered at age 12
Photo courtesy of Free The Children

Battled child labor, boy, 12, murdered

Islamabad, Pakistan (AP) - When Iqbal Masih was 4 years old, his parents sold him into slavery for less than $16.

For the next six years, he remained shackled to a carpet-weaving loom most of the time, tying tiny knots hour after hour.

By age 12, he was free and travelling the world in his crusade against the horrors of child labor.

On Sunday, Iqbal was shot dead while he and two friends were riding their bikes in their village of Muritke, 35 kilometres outisde the eastern city of Lahore. Some believe his murder was carried out by angry members of the carpet industry who had made repeated threats to silence the young activist.

Toronto Star, April 19, 1995.

It all began one ordinary weekday morning when I was 12. I was flipping through the local paper in search of my favorite comic strip, when a headline caught my attention. It read "Battled child labor, boy, 12, murdered." Intrigued by the fact that the boy in question was exactly my own age, I kept reading.

Appalled, I learned about the brutal conditions under which child laborer Iqbal Masih had worked for much of his short life. Sold into slavery at the age of 4, the Pakistani boy had spent six years chained to a carpet-weaving loom before making a miraculous escape and becoming an advocate for the rights of enslaved children everywhere. His success in promoting awareness about child labor prompted a carpet maker to have him killed.

Iqbal's story came as a profound shock to me, a middle-class Grade 7 student from Thornhill, Ontario. I was both stunned and sickened. In a single instant I realized that the world was a far different place from what I had always imagined it to be. Suddenly, I had so many questions that needed answers. What kind of people would sell their son? How could anybody get away with keeping a child prisoner? What exactly was child labor? Where was Pakistan?

Later that day I began to research the issue of child labor at my school library. To my horror, I discovered that in many parts of the world children exactly like me were forced to spend their days working in the most wretched conditions. While I sat in class, millions of children would only ever dream of going to school. It seemed unbelievable that I had never heard about any of this before. I wondered if I was the only one.

It's funny in saying it out loud and talking about the idea of starting a movement.

"With many people, their eyes kind of glaze over and they say, 'This is simply idealism,'—and it's true, and we are idealistic. We're shamelessly idealistic," Kielburger says.

"Most people said we were incredibly idealistic when we said we'd build one school, never mind 400 schools."

- Craig Kielburger (from *The London Free Press*)

Craig's Journey

Journal Excerpts
1995-1996

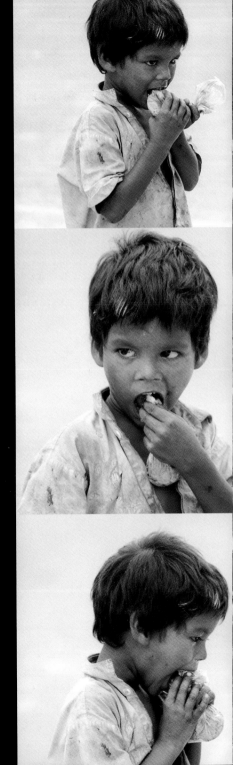

"Well, I arrived at 8:26 their time... There were coconut and banana trees! It was winter! We took a rickshaw rider from the airport to the home. The poverty is overwhelming; children are working in the street, picking up garbage, begging..." (Dhaka)

"Seeing first hand the lives of working children was my main reason for journeying to South Asia. But even I was not prepared for the abuse I would find in the back alleys of Bangkok. I don't think most adults would have been either." (Bangkok)

"The poverty that we found in parts of Bombay was overwhelming... In some parts of the city the homeless are so numerous that many are forced to walk the streets at night because the sidewalks are full of sleeping bodies." (Bombay)

"As we walked some children tagged along. What few clothes they had were dirt-stained and ragged. Most boys wore only shorts and the youngest wore nothing at all. Most had bare feet... I certainly stood out from the crowd... They whispered and giggled, daring each other to come close to me." (Dhaka)

"Kids have to be tough to survive on the streets of Kathmandu, where older gang members often beat and rob them. They face cold winters, hunger, homelessness, and unsympathetic police. But under each hard shell there is still a child." (Nepal)

"Mother Teresa asked me to write a message on a blackboard outside the chapel to remind the sisters to pray for labouring children. She moved me like no other person I have ever met. She held my hands in hers and looked into my eyes as if she were searching for my soul. 'The poor will teach you many things,' she said." (Calcutta)

"As we marched through the streets of Calcutta, we chanted, 'We want education!' and 'Stop child labour!' Many children on the march had seen their friends, or their own brothers and sisters, killed or severly injured in explosions at fireworks factories." (Calcutta)

"My final meal in India reminded me why I had come to South Asia. Seated with Shakif, a street vendor of my own age, I realized it was only a matter of luck that I had been born into a life of privilege, with all my needs met, while so many children around the world live in hardship." (Bombay)

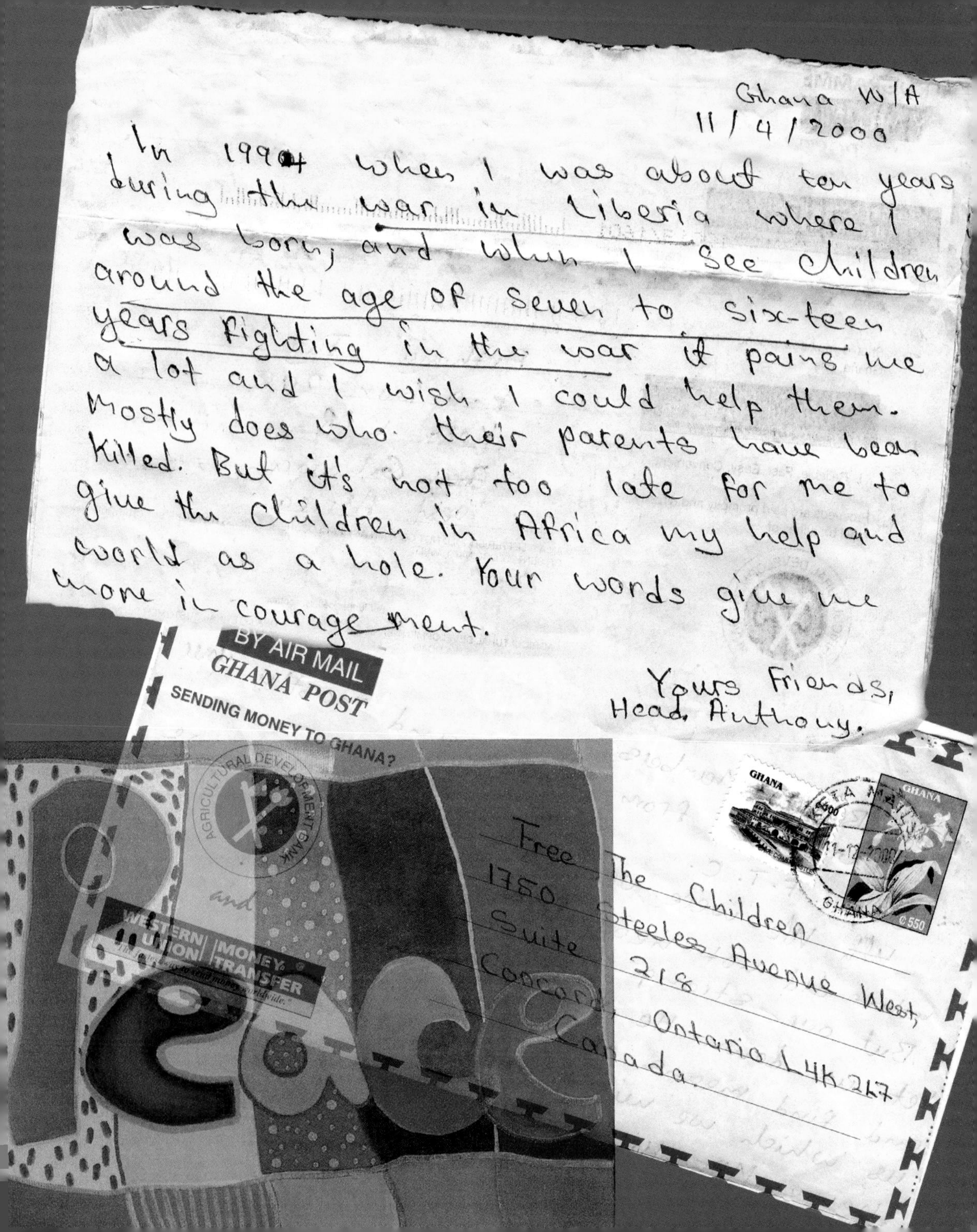

Ghana W/A
11/4/2000

In 1994 when I was about ten years during the war in Liberia where I was born, and when I see children around the age of seven to six-teen years fighting in the war it pains me a lot and I wish I could help them. Mostly does who their parents have been killed. But it's not too late for me to give the children in Africa my help and world as a hole. Your words give me more in courage ment.

Yours Friends,
Head, Anthony.

Free The Children
1750 Steeles Avenue West,
Suite 218
Concord Ontario L4K 2L7
Canada

GHANA
GHANA
11-12-2000

Marc's Spark

My involvement with social, environmental, and other issues first began in the most unlikely way.

I was a Grade 8 student in search of a science fair project. Science was definitely not one of my favorite subjects, and this was one assignment that I was looking forward to finishing up as quickly as possible. The only problem was, I couldn't even decide on a topic. I simply had no idea. I tried asking my mom, but she didn't have any ideas either.

No doubt spying an opportunity, my mother suggested I take my mind off of my troubles by helping with the household chores. As you can imagine, I was less than enthusiastic about spending my free time cleaning up around the house. But at least it wasn't science.

As I went to collect the cleaning products from under the sink, I happened to take a look at the labels plastered on the bottles—they all seemed to be filled with warnings! Bottle after bottle was marked HAZARDOUS and each bore the telltale skull and crossbones symbol. "Well," I thought to myself, "that settles it!" How could anybody be expected to clean the house with chemicals harmful to their health? What better reason could anyone have not to do the chores!

That afternoon I headed off to see my grandmother. As usual, I was eager to ask her questions about what things were like when she was my age—she always had some great stories to share! Remembering my earlier encounter with my mom's cleaning products, I asked her if she had had to use those chemicals growing up.

To my surprise, she told me that in her day, people had used things like vinegar and baking soda to make their homes sparkle. She was still reminiscing when several of her friends dropped by. They eagerly joined in our discussion, offering their favorite family recipes for cleaning products and arguing over who could provide the best tips! Everyone was determined to teach me how to clean things "properly." The debates grew pretty intense: everyone was convinced that their own methods were the only ones that could get the job done right.

19

Later that same week I decided to try out some of the recipes I had collected from my grandmother and her friends. I was curious to see whether simple, safe, household ingredients could really get things clean. I received permission to use a science lab at a local university, and I set to work testing various recipes. Before I knew it, I had found my science project!

HAZARDOUS PRODUCT SYMBOLS

Toxic or poisonous (can enter the body through ingestion, skin contact or inhalation)

Flammable (liquids that can ignite)

Explosive or Reactive (such as ammonia or bleach, that may create an explosion or release deadly vapours when mixed with other chemicals)

Corrosive (such as drain and oven cleaners, that eat away by chemical action and can burn living tissue on contact.)

These symbols show the **type** of hazard a product contains.

These geometric figures or frames show the **degree** of hazard. The more sides the frame has, the more dangerous the product.

Alternative Home Cleaners - Marc Kielburger

My project attracted far more attention than I could ever have imagined. I placed first in my school's science fair, and went on to compete in Canada's nationwide science fair. My project was named the best project at the fair! From there, things really took off. The Heinz Company agreed to print a booklet based on my project, filled with simple and useful recipes for alternative home cleaners. I began to speak to people about the importance of choosing environmentally friendly alternatives, becoming an advocate for environmental awareness. In trying to avoid some tiresome chores, I had discovered that I could actually make a difference in the world! Little did I know then that social involvement would become a lifelong passion.

Joe's Spark

(1983-2004)

I sometimes think about the person I used to be, and the life I lived. My family was a disaster zone and I counted down the days before I could escape. I recognized most of the police officers who patrolled my neighborhood—they had all taken turns visiting my house on numerous occasions. Fights, and the screaming and yelling that accompanied them, were a matter of routine in my home. My parents would repeatedly get "separated" in a game that often left my brothers and me alone and unsure of what would happen next.

It was even too much for my mom, a woman who had sacrificed almost everything she had—even her sanity—to make ends meet. She did her best to improve our family. We held dinners and tried to talk about our problems. But mostly shouting matches would emerge. Every day things only got worse. Twice my mom disappeared, and I was convinced I would never see her again.

My brother Bobby did manage to escape, if you could call it that. Social workers took him away and placed him in a group home. The day I found out that some of the other boys had pissed on his bed on his first night there I was outraged. When he ran away to the streets and became homeless, I knew it was a decision that I too would have made. Not too long after he chose the streets, someone shoved a lit cigarette up his nose and stole his last $5. I began to lose confidence and faith in the decency of people.

I left home at 17 on a spur-of-the-moment decision with nowhere to go. It was an act of desperation, but one I could not take back. Fortunately, after I'd resigned myself to nights in coffee shops, a friend took me in until I found a landlord who would rent to me even though I was underage. I took multiple jobs to support myself. Market research and telemarketing in the afternoons, waiting tables and deejaying at nights, and even dealing drugs to make spending money. I was still going to high school and trying to balance it all. One teacher kept telling me to stop blaming my problems on my home environment and take control of my life. They just didn't understand.

One day I met a kid named Jordan, a brilliant and funny person who came from a messed up home like mine. Jordan told me about a Free The Children camp that would "change my life."

My eyes started to glaze over.

Yeah, right, I thought. I don't think so. I started to turn away. "Did I tell you about the girls?" Jordan added. "There will be tons of girls. They come from all over the world..."

That's all I needed. Where do I sign up?

As I got to know the other youth at the camp, I noticed something different about them. They really cared. Not just about the social issues they were fighting for, but about everybody. And they offered me something that I thought only came with big money or a big knife: respect. I had a great time at the camp and decided to stay involved with Free The Children and this group of new friends. Slowly I started to get involved in their campaigns. Within a year I had made a decision that the drug dealing had to go. I realized that I would have to clean up my act, and say goodbye to many other things that had helped me to survive in the past.

I realized I had to live to a higher standard. Soon after I made this decision, I was fortunate enough to be sponsored to go with a group of young people to volunteer in the slums of Jamaica.

Riverton, Jamaica. I bounced down a country road in a bus with a group of volunteers, ready to "get involved." I stared out the windows. On either side of the bus were piles and piles of garbage. Suddenly one of the piles moved. A flap opened and out climbed a young boy and an old man. The flap of garbage was the front door to their home. Everyone on the bus went quiet. I felt my face; it was wet with tears.

Climbing out of the bus, we were surrounded by kids, all smiles and expectation. What could I do? I did the only thing I could think of: piggyback rides.

I could not get over how unreal the situation was. Here I was in the middle of a garbage dump with some of the poorest kids on earth. We were smiling. We were laughing.

It felt good.

Out of breath and seriously thirsty, I wandered over to a street vendor and

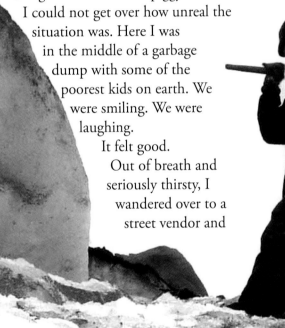

bought a carton of juice. As I raised it to my mouth, I noticed a small boy with big shining eyes staring at me. What was I thinking? Guilt quickly kept me from drinking the juice. I handed him the carton. "Here you go, kid, you can have it."

I expected a look of gratitude, but instead I watched the child's face turn serious. I watched him take a deep breath and then walk toward the other children, carton in hand. I couldn't believe my own eyes as I saw this incredibly cute and incredibly poor little boy making sure that each of his friends had an equal sip. By the time he had finally shared the juice with everyone, he walked over and offered me the carton before he took a sip of his own. To this day, I am left with the fact that I, a kid from North America, took a sip of juice before a 6-year-old kid who lived in a garbage dump.

I quickly realized that it wasn't all about me, after all. I wasn't the only victim. As bad as I had it, somebody always had it worse. And in this case, that somebody—a poverty-stricken little boy—wasn't ust surviving. He was living. This was a lesson I would never forget.

When I got home I decided to make some changes. I brought my family together and told them that I would be there for them—to help see us through hard times. I shared many of the stories from Jamaica and my past life with anyone who would listen. I spoke to my friends, to youth groups and even to schools. Soon I was offered a full-time job with Free The Children.

I am now a member of their speaking bureau and travel across North America to speak to

other young people about issues that concern them—youth violence, poverty, cultural diversity and service to others. I didn't realize how much impact my new life could have until the day I received a phone call at four in the morning.

The person on the other end of the line was crying. "I needed someone to talk to and I know you care about me," he said. "That's why I'm still alive."

I listened through his sobs as he told
me that he had just been standing on
the sidewalk, watching an approaching
bus, planning on jumping in front of
it and ending it all. At the last
minute, he'd stepped away and called
me instead. My little brother Bobby
told me that, thanks
to me, he would make
it through yet anothe
night.

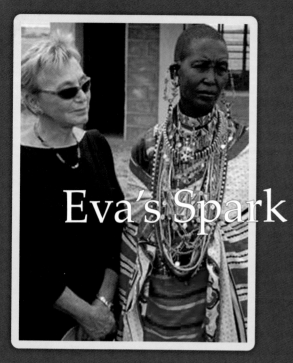

Eva's Spark

When I was 12 years old, my brother John, who was seven years my senior, took me on a clandestine mission. You see, it was wartime and the Nazis ruled our land. Those who resisted were instantly executed. Those who cooperated were rewarded with food stamps.

My brother John was part of the underground and risked his life daily to resist the savage occupation of our beloved country, Hungary, by the Nazis. I knew that John had a secret (even from our parents) and his trips every afternoon had a purpose. Often I would ask, "why can't I go with you?" and he just looked preoccupied and sent me on to read, or to play the accordion, an instrument we both loved dearly. He would say, "go practice and when I come back we will play a duet."

One afternoon upon my begging him more fiercely than usual, he gave in, and as soon as dusk spread on the horizon, we went off to the secret printing press where John and the other resistance members printed leaflets. Some leaflets urged Hungarians to rise up to fight against the Nazi oppressors, others would bring news gleaned from the "Voice of America and Radio Free Europe" about how and where the battles were raging.

There was a need to print and distribute daily because there was new information every day about the Nazi atrocities. There was also a constant danger that the hideout might be raided.

So that day, after the printing was finished, we distributed packets at different locations. The leaflets were picked up by our friends, who shared them with their friends, and so the network of resistance grew.

I was not aware of the danger we were in; nor could I predict that one day the group would be infiltrated by a spy or that John with many others would be rounded up and sentenced to death by hanging.

We were allowed to visit my brother twice during the next seven months. I will never forget the skeletal young man with the shaven head who was John. Nor will I ever forget the dirt, the insects, and the smells of the prison.

My parents were frantic. My father used all his powers, influence, and money to get John and the others out of jail. He hired lawyers, appealed to the court where he argued that it was just a youthful mistake, and asked for a general pardon.

After seven months of fear that we would be told that the punishment by hanging would be carried out, suddenly John was released. I never ever will forget his hunger for food, love, and his joy in playing his accordion. His fingers were stiff, his skin loose on his body, and his shaven head bloody from scratching the insect bites. John was home and it was the happiest day of my young life!

What was the next step for an activist who could not and would not stop his passion for freedom while gross injustices were facing us daily? John did what other young people attempted to do: join Tito and the Partisans in Yugoslavia and fight Hitler with guns not words, with strength, passion, and unity. We never talked about it, but knew instinctively what would be the next chapter in my brother's life.

One day he hugged me tight and asked me to be a good person, packed a few items of clothing and food, and kissed me. I sobbed so loud that John said I would bring in the Nazis. That made me lower my voice and I just cried silently, feeling an incredible void. Then he left.

John went the way many other young men did. He traveled at night with his four friends, and slept during the day in abandoned huts. One day, while hiding in a hut, they heard voices nearby and were discovered. John told his four friends to flee out the back and he would cover for them. It was one life against an army of soldiers. The Nazis won.

After the war was over, my mother traveled to the village from where the four friends had escaped. You see, all those who survived came back home and yet no word from John. As my mother came into the village, she stopped to talk with the villagers. While inquiring after my brother, she spotted a red and blue flannel shirt drying on a clothes line. John had worn that shirt when he left home and he never came back.

So, I became the activist I am because of John and all the other brothers and sisters who perished and for all the victims we witness every day of our lives.

- Eva Haller, U.S. Chair, Free The Children

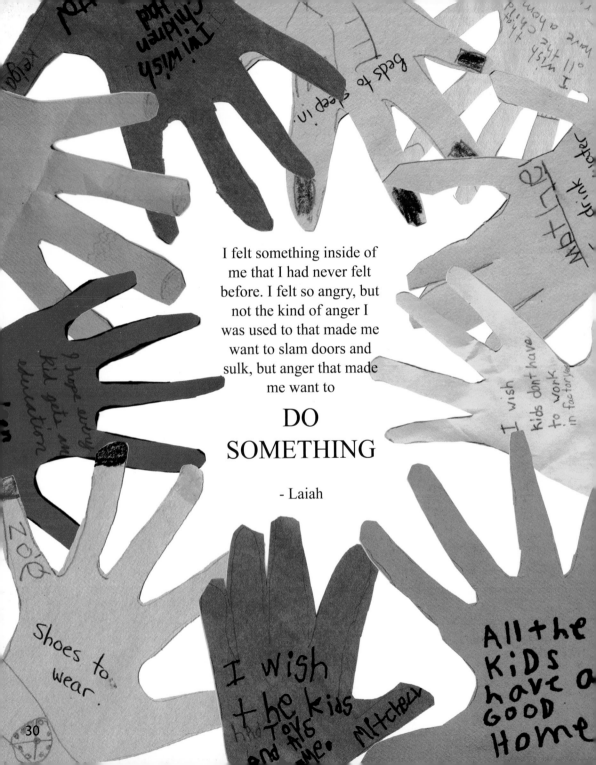

I felt something inside of me that I had never felt before. I felt so angry, but not the kind of anger I was used to that made me want to slam doors and sulk, but anger that made me want to

DO SOMETHING

- Laiah

Many adults have built within their wall a notion that young people make

TOO MuCH NoiSE

They would be convinced that the best solution is to use their wall to shut the noise out. Today, I stood with my ear to the wall of my jail cell and heard the encouragement of the children. Although I had been scratching at a dent in the wall with my tool, the shouts seemed to be coming from the ceiling.

The **shoUts** caused **VIBRATIONS.**

The **VIBRATIONS** created **cracks.**

It was a sunny day outside.

The sky was the limit.

-Joe Opatowski

ED'S SPARK

"It is as a witness to hope, courage, and action that I become inspired. Every time I hear someone speak, I think. Every time I see someone act, I believe. And every time I act—by speaking out against racism or homophobia, by eating a delicious vegan meal, by giving to someone in need, by sharing myself and my hugs, and by living simply—I feel full of hope and courage to act again. No one event can start a revolution, but any action could."

- Ed Gillis

"To pinpoint a single 'spark'
in a lifetime of activism is
like finding fish in a lake:
they're all around you, some
bigger than others but all
key parts of the ecosystem."
- Ed Gillis

"But what has sparked
me to action time and
again is action itself. It
was watching people
stand by their values and
live their message."
- Ed Gillis

If we just take one S T E P

at a time—one battle at a time—we can make a difference in the world. Even if my activism just helps take one child out of a factory, it will all have been worth it. For the future of tomorrow's generation begins with a step from our generation.

- Neera Singal

Artwork by Christopher Harley

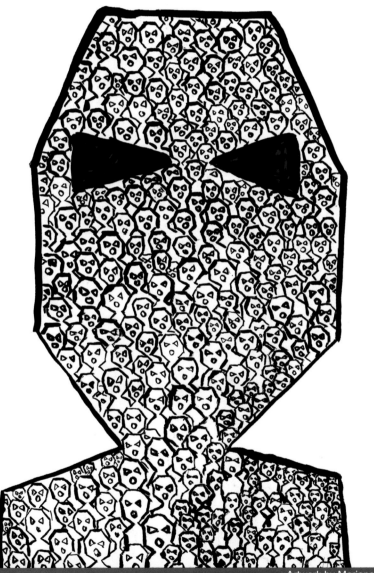

Artwork by Mariana Wagner

Screams that we do not hear.

There is only one way
To help those in need,
And that is for us all to work
    together
And start planting a seed.

A seed that will grow
Into a large, sturdy tree,
That will end world hunger
Among children like you and me.

-Sarah P

Artwork by Alamgir Mondal

ACE!
ACE!
ACE!

It there is no peace. There would not be a beautiful sunset.

Crystal Lynn

PEACE

one wants to live in this

This is what everyone wants.

The seven need in peace

ace is what all we eed! Carla Eges

We ♥ need 🕊 Peace! ♥
Jahns

Stephanie G5W
B3
G5 McKenzie Rm. 222 PEACE PUZZLE
PEACE
PEACE IS NOT FIGHTING!!!
Alanna
Cliff Low

HE WORLD OF PEACE!
PEACE
PEACE

Peace over the world

Peace Rules

Felicia

we need peace

Peace

Peace means no war

W A R
PEACE

Peace we need peace!

Chloe

37

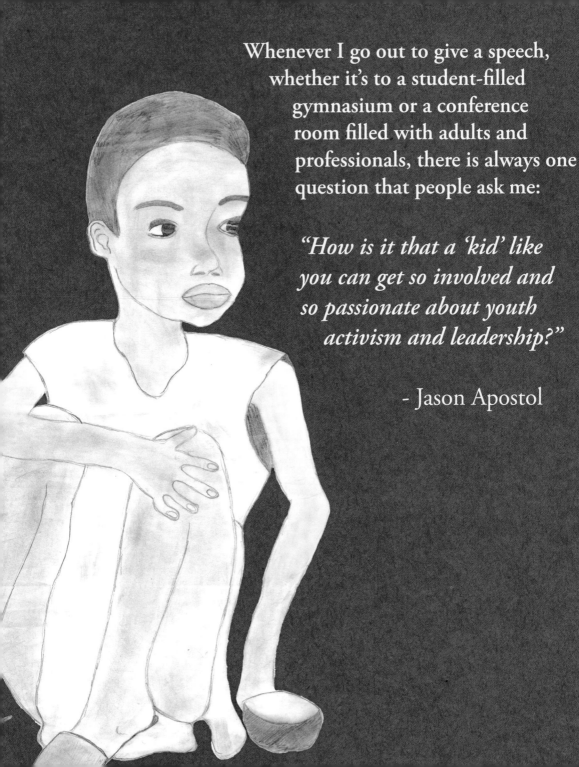

Whenever I go out to give a speech, whether it's to a student-filled gymnasium or a conference room filled with adults and professionals, there is always one question that people ask me:

"How is it that a 'kid' like you can get so involved and so passionate about youth activism and leadership?"

- Jason Apostol

I have a dream that nobody Would play With Guns.
By Alex Courtemanche

I have a dream that everybody is nice to animals. Michael Watkins

I have a dream to Be a fireman So I can help People. BY, Curtis Brown

I have a dream that everybody is kind to each other. By, Amanda Yates

I have a dream that we all have food. By, Levi Stephens

I have a dream to be a Singer when I grow up and make people happy. by, Seleah Scoma

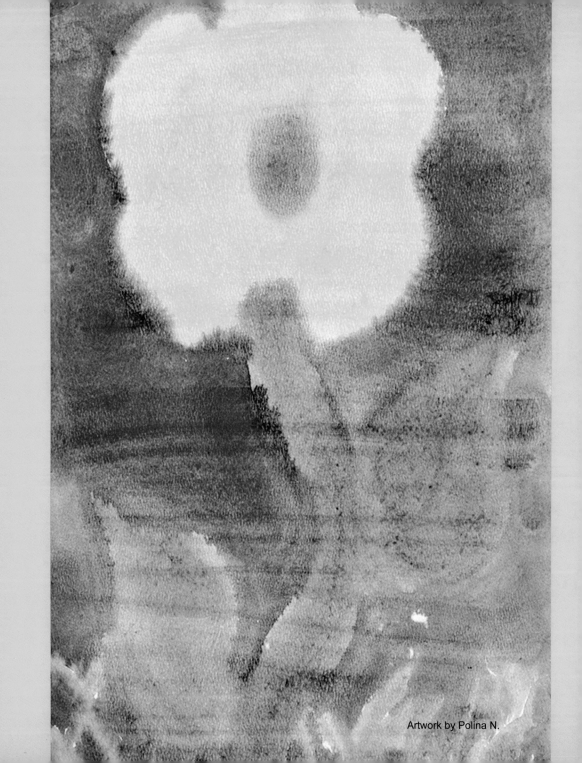

Artwork by Polina N.

Sitting in my little university townhouse with the television on, finished with my morning restaurant job, I looked out into the beautiful day and back to the neon television.

I looked down at myself and envisioned what I would look like from an outsider's perspective: sitting there, all alone, staring hypnotically at a metal box, while the sun beamed outside and the breeze blew.

All of a sudden, I felt more like an android than a human being. I thought of all the times in my life when I'd wasted whole days "vegging" in front of the television…

All the while missing life.

Paralyzed.

Comatose.

Oblivious.

That was it…a moment of revelation that told me how much I was disrespecting LIFE.

- Louise Kent

You are no longer only citizens of our cities, states, or countries.

Artwork by Ms. Weeks's
Grade 8 Class

You are now truly citizens of the world.

- Craig Kielburger

Roxanne's Spark

My first time outside of North America, I spent six months in Klong Toey, one of the most destitute slums in Bangkok, Thailand. A volunteer at the Human Development Center, I worked with women and children afflicted with HIV/AIDS. Years later, bittersweet memories of my experiences remain etched in my mind. There is one that will forever have a place of its own.

Nan was a 3-year-old girl diagnosed with full-blown AIDS. When I first met her, she was sitting cross-legged on a patchwork of scrap vinyl flooring, part of the makeshift shelter she called home. When I spoke her name in greeting, she could barely even turn her shaven head in my direction. By then, the disease had deprived her of the energy she would have needed to make this simple gesture.

I will never forget this little girl who stubbornly spit out the chicken and vegetables we tried to feed her in the hospital cafeteria. She much preferred her grandmother's rice and rice water, her family's staple meal. Though she suffered terribly, her tiny body housed a defiant spirit that fought her disease until the end. Her determination profoundly affected me, a healthy young Canadian who had never been forced to struggle in this way. **It was a spark powerful enough to ignite my own sense of resolve.**

By the time Marc and I returned to Canada after spending a year volunteering abroad, Free The Children had become a grassroots phenomenon. The organization was searching for its first staff members in a bid to manage an overwhelming workload.

As a network of children helping children, it represented a fresh new approach to global challenges that many people were immediately drawn to. At the time, resources were scarce, and the challenges enormous. Few of us had much experience with running a charitable organization, let alone one with global aspirations. We may not have had much in the way of funding, office space or equipment, but the one thing we did have in abundance was determination.

Ten years later, I count myself lucky to have been part of so many of Free The Children's "firsts"—whether organizing our first youth conference, launching our leadership camp, leading a group of young activists through India, or most recently, establishing an education center in Kenya.

As Free The Children continues to grow, I am honored to take on new and different roles within the organization—all of which I undertake with the same determination and resolve which I remember and continue to admire in Nan.

- Roxanne Joyal

The Story of Amandla and Sibusiso

I would like to tell you the story of Amandla and Sibusiso. Don't know them? Sure you do—they may be more familiar than you think. Sibusiso was happy, content with his life. In fact, some may say he was quite occupied with his life. Paddling down the river of life he was confronted by a fork in the path. There was a signpost lodged in a small island between the two streams with two arrows pointing in either direction. One arrow read Ukungazi and the other Ulwazi.

Not pausing for a moment, Sibusiso paddled to the right, the Ukungazi way, merely because he saw no difference between the two and he was occupied with a particularly juicy bit of gossip he had heard the night before. It didn't seem to matter which way he took.

Along the same river of life came Amandla, who soon reached the signpost. Amandla was perplexed: she knew there had to be a reason for the fork in the path (as nothing along the river so far had been a coincidence). She rowed her canoe up to the little island and looked carefully at the two waterways. She noticed that the Ukungazi way was calm, and the surrounding scenery was beautiful in an idyllic, bland sort of way. Ulwazi, on the other hand, seemed a more difficult path.

As beautiful as the Ukungazi, the water here was rougher and Amandla could see several large rocks up ahead. She suspected that the muted roar she heard in the distance was a waterfall. After a few minutes of deliberation, she picked up her paddle and steered her little canoe to the left. She could never resist a challenge…

The moral of the story? I'm sure you can discern it yourself, given a few translations. My passion is Africa, and a recent journey to South Africa introduced me to the Zulu people and language. Amandla, Sibusiso, Ulwazi and Ukungazi are all Zulu words:

> Amandla = Power
> Sibusiso = Bliss
> Ulwazi = Knowledge
> Ukungazi = Ignorance

You see, you *do* know Amandla and Sibusiso after all, and it was no coincidence that Amandla was compelled toward Ulwazi and Sibusiso chose the path of Ukungazi.

Free The Children helped me to make my choice by teaching me to look for the differences in the two rivers.

- Sheena Kamal

The people of Klong Toey—from the street vendors to the primary school teachers to the AIDS patients—taught me so much. Amidst the wretchedness of the slums, I found countless examples of beauty and generosity.

And among the orphaned boys and girls who survived abandonment and molestation and things no child should have to go through, I found an inner strength that I can only hope to develop within myself.

- Sonya Hetrick

the work

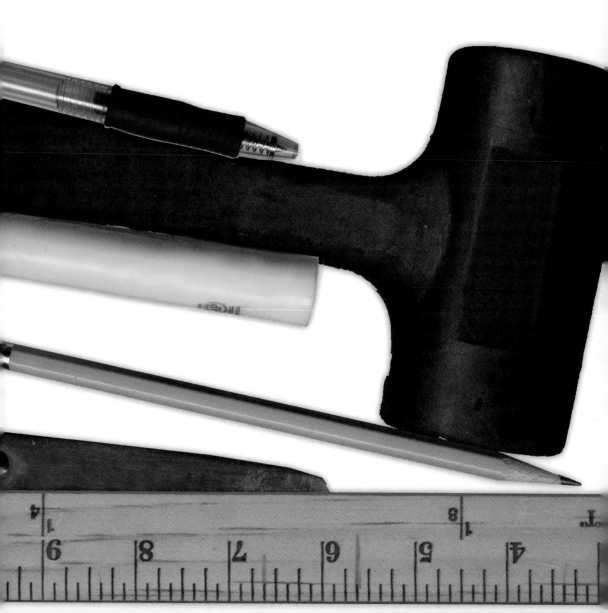

What follows from your SPARK is what you do with it: your WORK. Defined as "sustained physical or mental effort to overcome obstacles and achieve an objective or result," work is different for different individuals. And when your work is motivated by the SPARK to HELP other people, all work is important and HELPFUL.

Welcome Volunteers

I'm little too, too short and Stout.

today's youth

today's leaders

The poems, stories, drawings and letters show what excites kids, makes them want to act, and emboldens them to create a difference. Words and artwork change us because they move us. Now that you've identified your spark, you may wonder what to do next. What work should you do?

Our dream is to one day be out of work and not to have to come and do our work anymore.

Essentially, the dream is to throw ourselves out of work.

So that 250 million kids involved in child labor are no longer in child labor.

So that 113 million kids who can't afford to go to school and never stepped foot inside a classroom will have a chance to have an education.

www.freethec...

whichever type of work you do first, you can start right now. As Anne Frank said, "How wonderful it is that nobody need wait a single moment before starting to improve the world."

Kids Can Free The Children

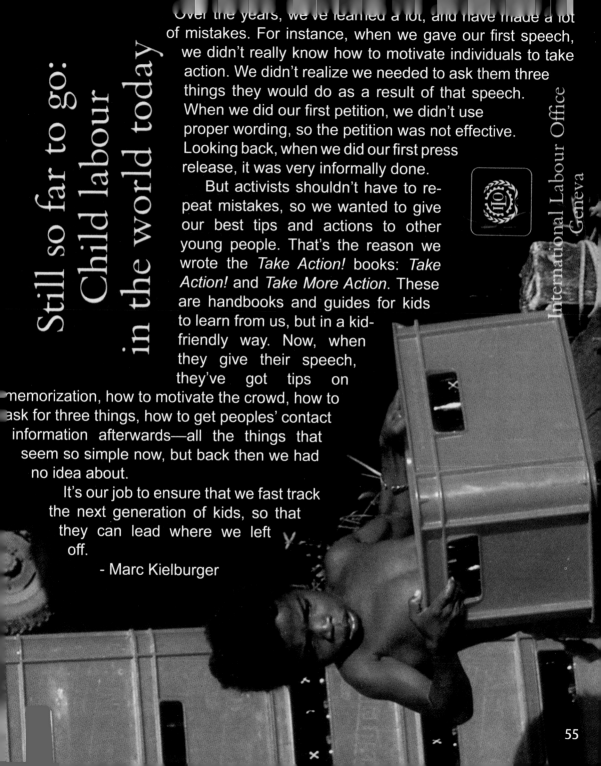

Still so far to go: Child labour in the world today

Over the years, we've learned a lot, and have made a lot of mistakes. For instance, when we gave our first speech, we didn't really know how to motivate individuals to take action. We didn't realize we needed to ask them three things they would do as a result of that speech. When we did our first petition, we didn't use proper wording, so the petition was not effective. Looking back, when we did our first press release, it was very informally done.

But activists shouldn't have to repeat mistakes, so we wanted to give our best tips and actions to other young people. That's the reason we wrote the *Take Action!* books: *Take Action!* and *Take More Action*. These are handbooks and guides for kids to learn from us, but in a kid-friendly way. Now, when they give their speech, they've got tips on memorization, how to motivate the crowd, how to ask for three things, how to get peoples' contact information afterwards—all the things that seem so simple now, but back then we had no idea about.

It's our job to ensure that we fast track the next generation of kids, so that they can lead where we left off.

- Marc Kielburger

International Labour Office
Geneva

A Difference Can Be Made If We SAY "NO" To CHILD LABOR

Artwork by Corine Wong

KIDS ARN'T SLAVES,

THEY'RE THE FUTURE

Craig's Story

I walked to the front and turned to face the 30 students in my class. The room was silent except for a couple of boys whispering in a back row. When I began they, too, were quiet. But I was still nervous; I always found speaking in front of my peers a tough thing to do, and I still had no idea how they would react to what I would say.

"I was wondering if anyone saw this article on the front page of last Wednesday's *Toronto Star*," I began.

I had made photocopies of it, which I passed around the classroom. As I did so, I started to tell Iqbal's story. I described his struggles and his dream, and how that dream had been cut short by an assassin's bullet. I presented the alarming statistics on child labor. As I spoke, I could see that many of my classmates were just as shocked as I was by the story. Anger, sympathy and disbelief filled the room.

"So this is the issue," I said. "I don't know a lot about it, but I want to learn more. Maybe some of us could start a group to look at it together." And then came the fateful question, "Who wants to join?"

About 18 hands shot up, and I very quickly jotted down their names. I thanked Mr. Fedrigoni and the class for the half hour of their time I had taken.

And through that simple action, it began.

At lunchtime that day, some of us got together and talked about what we could do. I was amazed at how enthusiastic they all were. I told them about the youth fair on Friday.

"Do you think we could put together a display?" I asked. "We haven't got much time."

"Sure. Let's do it."

"We can all meet at my house," I said.

That night, 12 of us got together. It was a very tight deadline, with just two days to prepare. We found an old science-fair board, and we covered it with colored paper, pasting on all the information I had found on child labor in the library, then drawing pictures to illustrate it.

We had determined that our first objective should be to inform people of the plight of child laborers. Armed with such knowledge, they might be willing to help. We decided to draw up a petition to present to the government, and called on the expertise of a couple of human-rights groups to refine the wording for us.

But we were still without a name for our group. For more than an hour we struggled to come up with something suitable. We flipped through the newspaper clippings for inspiration. One of them reported on a demonstration in Delhi, India, where 250 children had marched through the streets with placards, chanting, "We want an education," "We want freedom," "Free the children!"

"That's it!" someone shouted. "Free The Children!"

"Perfect," I said. "We're using their words. Children speaking for children."

"Exactly."

We had found a name. Marilyn Davis, the best artist among us, had earlier drawn a picture of children chained to a carpet loom. Before pasting the picture onto our information board, across the top she had written slogans, including "Break the Chains" and "Save the Children." Now we pasted a piece of paper over the word "SAVE" and wrote "FREE" in big letters.

Free The Children was born. We hoisted our board, like a giant placard, in solidarity with the children who had marched through the streets of Delhi.

I remember lying awake that Thursday night, thinking about what we had gotten ourselves into. Here we were, just a group of friends, a ragtag lot compared to all the other organizations sure to be taking part in the youth fair. Yet we had worked hard, read all the information I had collected, and felt confident we could get our point across to anyone who was willing to listen.

As I slowly drifted off to sleep, I could only think, ready or not, here we go. And the next morning, that's exactly what happened—off we went, the start of something that would take over my life and catch the world's attention to an extent that none of us could ever have imagined.

- Craig Kielburger

Kleine Hände, Kleine Fäuste.

HELFT DEN KINDERN DIESER WELT

Small Hands, Small Fists.
Help the Children of This World

A Child's Joy Shouldn't Come

From Another Child's Toil

Documention:
Know Your Source

As you research, write down all the bibliographial information about your sources. Check where the author got his or her material. If you can support your statements with solid facts, you will be confident in sharing what you learned.

Consider Both Sides

Make sure you have the whole story.

How To Be A Critical Reader

Do Not Believe Everything You Read

When doing research, it is important to compare different sources before you accept as true what one book says. Do not be impressed with words just because they are in print.

Beware of Bias

Whether or not they are conscious of it, all writers have a different point of view, also known as a bias.

Get Others Involved.

do some investigating

Tackle one thing at a time

Choose A Direction

Researching Made Easy!!!!!

Organize Your Information

Ask the experts

contact organizations

Set a goal and a deadline

Dear Free The Children

    In science we are doing child labor and we are reading your
book. My class did a fundraiser by doing a chocolate sale to raise
money and donate it to you. My class would like the money we are
giving to the project you are on, when all the kids go to this place
and get education and 3 meals a day.

    When I am at the table eating I sometimes don't eat all of my food
but know that we are talking about child labor and how they only
get like 1 meal a day and I get 3 and if I waste food like they
would love to be me because i get lots of food and i even get
snacks between each meal. I am trying not to waste food anymore.

Yours Truly
    Jessica .S.

Dear Free the Children Organisation,

    My class has been reading about child labour f
awhile and we decided to raise money from
chocolate sales to give to your organisation. We
were reading the book Free the Children. It is an
amazing book. It's wonderful that your
organisation is helping children. My class is putting
on an assembly on what child labour is and how to
help stop it. We hope our donation will help.

                                            Sincerely,
                                        Kelsey McPhail

Hi crig! My name is Eritha I live in PeachLan
B.C. I'm 10 years of age. I'm writing to you
because my class is reading your book Free the
children, as well as well had a choclate sak
and rased adout 160.00 Dollars to be put
towards a medical senter. . . . . so yey

66

May 22, 2003.

Dear Free the Children Foundation,

Hi, I'm a grade 5 student from Holy Name Catholic School. As a grade 5 and 6 group, we read some excerpts from "Free the Children" by Craig Kielberger. Together we researched some Social Justice issues, like sweatshops. We then went into groups made up of some grade 5's and 6's. Each group got to present to a grade from our school (grades 1-8). Depending on the grade we got, we had to make them understand about social justice. We mostly focused on telling them about sweatshops. We explained why we were doing this, and gave each grade a different coloured piece of paper. They traced their handprints and marked off what they could do for social justice on a checklist, for example, if they could be kind to everyone or donate food to the poor. After all of the handprints were completed, we made a banner with all the hands on it that said, "Holy Name Works For Justice."

On May 2, 2003 we had a No-Logo day, where the students were asked to avoid wearing logos, and make $1.00 donation to the Free the Children Foundation. Holy Name School collected $130.00 to donate to F.T.C.

We think what you are doing is very worthwhile. We hope that this money will make a difference!

Sincerely,
Grade 5 and Grade 6 Students From,
Holy Name Catholic School,
Welland, Ontario.

The United Nations Convention on the Rights of the Child

The U.N. Convention on the Rights of the Child is an international human rights treaty about young people. It has been adopted by more countries than any other international human rights treaty. By January 1996, 187 countries (excluding the United States and Somalia) had signed or ratified it.

The U.N. Convention describes the basic things that governments owe to people under 18 years of age. It can be divided into four groups of rights:

I. Playing a Part means being included in decisions, freedom to join with others, freedom to express ourselves and freedom to receive information from lots of sources.

II. Reaching our Potential includes the things we need to develop as best as we can. This group lists the importance of education, family, culture and identity in our lives.

III. Living Well: Our Right to Survival includes all our more basic needs. This includes food and shelter, our standard of living and our health.

IV. Being Free from Harm allows for young people to be protected from many things, including abuse, neglect, economic exploitation, torture, abduction and prostitution.

I. PLAYING A PART: OUR RIGHT TO PARTICIPATE

Article 3 Our Best Interests as Young People- Our best interests should be considered first and foremost.

Article 12 Having Our Opinions Heard- We have the right to make our views known in decisions that affect us.

Article 14 Our Freedom of Conscience and Religion- We have the right to freedom of thought and religion.

Article 15 Our Freedom of Association- We have the right to meet with others, and to join or start an association.

Article 16 Our Freedom from Invasions of Privacy- We have the right to be free from invasions of our privacy.

Article 17 The Media- Governments have the responsibility to make sure information is available to us.

II. REACHING OUR POTENTIAL: DEVELOPING WHO WE ARE

Article 5 Respect for Parents- Governments must respect the rights of parents, extended family and guardians.
Article 7 Our Name and Nationality- The right to a name, nationality and to be cared for by our parents.
Article 23 Disabled Young People- The right to special care and education that will help achieve self-reliance.
Article 28 Our Education- We have the right to education and to help eliminate ignorance and illiteracy.
Article 30 Being from a Minority Group- We have the right to enjoy our culture, religion and our own language.

III. LIVING WELL: OUR RIGHT TO SURVIVAL

Article 6 Survival and Development- The right to life, survival and development to the maximum extent.
Article 9 Separation from Parents- We have the right to live with our parents and not to be separated from them.
Article 24 Health Care- We have the right to the highest level of health and medical care attainable.
Article 27 Our Standard of Living- We have the right to an adequate standard of living for our well-being.

IV. BEING FREE FROM HARM: OUR RIGHT TO PROTECTION

Article 2 Freedom from Discrimination- The Convention applies to all young people without exception.
Article 32 Child Labour-The right to be protected from economic exploitation that is a threat to our well-being.
Article 33 Protection from Narcotics- The right to be protected from the use and distribution of illegal drugs.
Article 34 Protection from Sexual Exploitation- Protection from sexual abuse, prostitution and pornography.
Article 37 Punishment and Detention- We have the right to protection from torture, cruelty and unlawful arrest.
Article 40 Young People and Justice- The right to be presumed innocent and the right to a fair trial.

OPINION

Stop child exploitation by shopping with a conscience

His say

By Craig Kielburger
SPECIAL TO THE TRIBUNE

I am a 13-year-old boy who lives in a suburb of Toronto, and like other kids my age I enjoy basketball and Nintendo. My parents are both teachers. We have a nice house, and I have never gone hungry a day in my life. Before April 17, 1995, I did not know very much about where my running shoes or soccer balls were made, or who made them.

But an article that I read in the Toronto Star while I was having breakfast that day changed everything. It was a story about a Pakistani boy named Iqbal Masih, who at age 4 was sold into slavery for less than $15. He was shackled to a carpet loom for up to 12 hours each day, six days a week. With his little hands he tied thousands of tiny knots. He was paid 3 cents a day.

After six years of slave-like labor, Iqbal escaped. He was a natural leader, and he began a campaign against the exploitation of Pakistani girls and boys by unscrupulous owners of carpet factories and brick kilns. His heroic efforts earned him the Reebok Human Rights Award, which was presented to him in Boston in December 1995. He was promised a scholarship at an American university. But at age 12, Iqbal was murdered not far from his home outside Lahore, Pakistan.

Craig Kielburger is founder of Free the Children, a children's-rights advocacy organization.

I was the same age as Iqbal when he was killed, and his death upset me very much. I asked my mom what I could do to help Iqbal's cause. With my friends I started researching the issue of child labor around the world, and what we learned shocked us. We decided to form an organization made up of school-age children around the world who want to end the exploitation of kids our age.

According to the latest report of the International Labor Organization, more than 120 million girls and boys 5 to 14 living in developing countries work full-time. Few of them go to school. In India, children are employed in workshops, garages and small factories making matches, fireworks and glass. They often work up to 15 hours each day in hazardous conditions. In Thailand and the Philippines, a virtual industry has grown up around the girls and boys who are used in the sex trade. In Sudan, destitute children are rounded up, beaten, shackled and auctioned off to the highest bidder.

You may be saying: "Well this is far away, in another country. What does this have to do with me?" American consumers may unknowingly be part of the problem. Poor children in many countries are employed in the textile, sporting-goods and toy industries, making products that may eventually end up on the shelves of North American stores. By buying these products, we may be contributing to the exploitation of children.

Child labor is a complex problem, and there are no easy answers. Legislation on its own simply won't work. Ensuring that all children have access to free primary schooling is the most effective means of protecting children from abuse. Unfortunately, many countries invest more money in Western-manufactured weapons (including equipment made in the U.S. and Canada) than they do in primary schooling.

But it is also very important that consumers around the world have information about how goods are made so they can make responsible choices when buying toys or running shoes for their own children.

Until recently, product labeling has been basic and difficult to police. Now, thanks to a promising development called Rugmark, there is hope that consumers can be better informed than ever. Supported by private voluntary organizations and carpet manufacturers in India and Pakistan, the Rugmark labeling system ensures that people buying carpets will not be walking on the dreams of children. Each carpet comes with the distinctive Rugmark logo, and with a guarantee that shows that the carpet is an authentic, child-labor-free product. Manufacturers who join Rugmark agree to unannounced inspections of their looms by child-advocacy groups.

Rugmark is a success story, and it is being copied by manufacturers in other sectors. Reebok Corp. announced that it is guaranteeing that all soccer balls produced with the Reebok logo will be child-labor free. This is believed to be the first time a guarantee of this kind has been placed on a widely distributed consumer product. Reebok will put in place a tough monitoring program to ensure that children are not employed in places where their soccer balls are made.

Companies do pay attention to consumer pressure. Corporations must be challenged to take steps to provide adequate labeling of all products. As a child, I am particularly concerned about toys made in sweatshops in Southeast Asia. Can the people at Toys 'R' Us and Sears assure us that all the toys they sell are child-labor free? Have Mattel and Hasbro ever considered a Toymark for their products that will guarantee that they have not been made from the exploitation of children? What will it take to make them move on this issue?

With the holiday shopping season in full swing, Americans should consider rewarding those companies that are interested in making a difference, as well as making money. Levi Straus has for years been very concerned about human-rights issues and has closed its factories in China. Ben and Jerry's goes out of its way to provide employment for homeless people in their ice-cream stores. The Body Shop has a tradition of supporting local charities and environmental causes.

Kids should ask more questions about those $150 running shoes that they want their parents to buy. Having the same shoes as Michael Jordan may be important, but so is protecting girls and boys who have no toys to play with. Encourage your children to write to manufacturers and ask this simple question: Can they guarantee that no children were employed in the making of the products they sell?

Companies and governments must take steps now to ensure that kids go to school in the morning, rather than to the fireworks factory or the brick kiln. I have spoken with working children in Pakistan, in India and in Brazil, and I have asked them what they want to do. They tell me their dream is to be in school, to learn to read and write. They want to be like other kids.

Robert Kennedy is one of my heroes. Recently, at the launch of Rugmark in Canada, I had the opportunity to meet his daughter, Kerry Kennedy-Cuomo. She reminded me that the most important message from her father was that people can make a difference, that "history is shaped by individual acts of courage and belief."

American adults and children have the power to change the world—if they choose to get involved. I challenge girls and boys across America to turn off their televisions, to get out their pen and turn on their computers and continue the campaign that was started by a poor boy in Pakistan who had no possessions to his name. Remember, we are young, but we are many!

For more information on Free the Children, write to 16 Thorn bank Rd., Thornhill, Ontario, Canada L4J2A2, or call 905-881-0__. Or e-mail the group at freechildclo.com or visit its Web site at h__ /www.freethechildren.org.

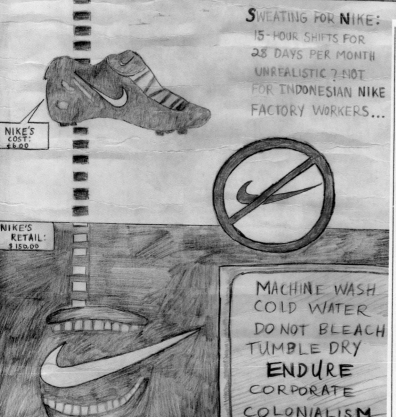

JUST STOP IT.

SWEATING FOR NIKE:
15-HOUR SHIFTS FOR
28 DAYS PER MONTH
UNREALISTIC? NOT
FOR INDONESIAN NIKE
FACTORY WORKERS...

NIKE'S
COST:
$6.00

NIKE'S
RETAIL:
$150.00

MACHINE WASH
COLD WATER
DO NOT BLEACH
TUMBLE DRY
ENDURE
CORPORATE
COLONIALISM

THERE IS NO FINISH LINE

Artwork by Charles Mizrahi

David Middlecamp/Telegram-Tribune

PROTEST: Members of the Free the Children club at Paso Robles High School collect Nike sportswear to be shipped back to the company's headquarters in Oregon.

Students give Nike the boot

PASO ROBLES

By Jeff Ballinger
Telegram-Tribune

In a crusade highlighting the alleged human rights abuses of the Nike Corp., a high school club is asking the sporting goods goliath to "Just don't do it."

The Free the Children club at Paso Robles High School organized a boycott this week, collecting from their classmates 14 pairs of new and used Nike shoes and numerous shirts and sweatshirts.

Club president Maria Campoverde, a junior, said the goods were to be shipped back Friday to Nike headquarters in Beaverton, Or., to Chief Executive Officer Phil Knight. A letter enclosed asked Knight to change his company's employment practices in southeast Asia regarding children and young adults.

The 2-year-old local club has about 20 members, and is a chapter of an international children's organization dedicated to protecting children from exploitation and abuse. It even has a web site at http://www.slocs.k12.ca.us/pasohigh/children/freethechildren.html.

It is one of several groups worldwide calling for the better treatment of Nike's overseas workers.

During lunch Friday, club members and adviser Stan Cooper, a social science teacher, handed out leaflets to students detailing how the

See **NIKE**, Back Page

Sunday, December 7, 2003, at 2:00 p.m.

At the home of Mrs. Leonore Meyer
240 East 62nd Street, New York

Children Will Listen (from *Into the Woods*)   Stephen Sondheim
            Angela Rose Bryan-Brown

Royal March of the Lion (from *Carnaval des animaux*)   Camille Saint-Saëns
            Raymond Blackenhorn

In the Hall of the Mountain King   Edvar Grieg
            Gautam Bhagat

Clair de Lune   Claude Debussy
            Angela Cheng

Grande Valse Brillante   Frédéric Chopin
            Audrey Juok Kwon

Gymonpédie No. 3   Erik Satie
Mrs. Robinson   Paul Simon
            Sabrina Ali

Breathe   Holly Lamar & Stephanie Bentley
            Ayesha Bhagat

Jesu, Joy of Man's Desiring   Johann Sebastian Bach
            Molly Colman

Gavotte   Johann Sebastian Bach
            Zachary Medina

Prelude in C Major   Johann Sebastian Bac[h]
            Matthew Brock

Minuet in G Major   Johann Sebastian [Bach]
Toymaker's Dance   Anom[
            Kafi Mavour

Toccata in D minor   Johann Seba[stian Bach]
            Juliet Bryan-Brown

Sorcerer's Apprentice
            J.Y. Song

July 8, 2002.

Hunter College High School KCFTC Chapter,
c/o Juliet Bryan-Brown and Sabrina Ali
1755 York Avenue, Apt. 21C,
New York, NY 10128 - 6827

Dear Juliet, Sabrina and members of the Hunter College High School KCFTC Chapter,

Greetings from Kids Can Free the Children! I am writing to inform you that we have recently received your generous donation of $1235 US, which you so creatively raised through your Benefit Concert. You did an amazing job! Thanks so much for your hard efforts on behalf of children living in less fortunate circumstances.

As per your request, we will be forwarding these funds to your partner school in the community of San Pedro Las Ballas 2, in Waslala, Nicaragua. They will be surprised and thrilled to find out that you still remember them!

I will also remind them that you are very axious to hear from the teacher and especially the students. Hopefully, this contact will forge a long lasting relationship with those children you care so much about.

Please do not hesitate to contact me, or John Gaither, our School Building Coordinator, if you have any more questions about your donation or your partner school. I may be reached at kits@freethechildren.com or (905) 760-9382.

Have a great summer!

Sincerely,

Paz Gajardo
Projects Coordinator

c.c.   John Gaither, School Building Coordinator
            files

ST. MARY'S ROMAN CATHOLIC SCHOOL

P.O. Box 480, Sexsmith, Alberta T0H 3C0
Tel: 568-3631   Fax: 568-3835

May 4, 2004

Dear Generous Business Owner,

My name is Mrs. Bonnie Anderson and I am writing on behalf of my grade two class at **St. Mary's Catholic School** in Sexsmith. I am writing to you today to share an exciting opportunity. We would like your business to support our class project by **donating financially to our cause so that we can have the book that we created published in color (as opposed to black and white)**. You donated generously last year and wondered if we could count on your support again.

We are currently studying the issue of **child labour** around the world. We have done a lot of research on this topic and are now trying to spread the message. We are also fundraising $800 to print our book in color. This is a story about a child from Sexsmith who travels to Sierra Leone. The books will be sold after being printed as a fundraiser for Free the Children.

We also collected school and health kit supplies to support our sister school that was built through a Canadian organization called **Free The Children**, which was founded by a 12-year-old boy named Craig Kielburger. Craig is currently attending University in Toronto in International Studies and was recently nominated for a Nobel Peace Prize. Amazingly, he **came to Grande Prairie** to accept a donation last May of over $24,000! That was how we helped fund the building of the primary school was built in Sierra Leone, Africa.

There are approximately **250 million child labourers** around the world. These are children who live in extreme poverty. We feel that they need to be **learning and not labouring**. We have been inspired by one such boy, Iqbal Masih, who was sold into slavery at four years of age for only $12. Eventually, he was rescued and chose to speak out against the horrors of child labour. For this, he was murdered Easter Sunday, 1995 while riding his bike with his cousins. Therefore, **twelve** has become an important number in our study and this is why we are **challenging people to donate twelve dollars or multiples of twelve dollars**. Grande Prairie is a generous city that has many blessings. We know that with your help we **can and will make a difference** in the world.

Would you please consider helping our class? In return for your generosity we would like to offer you a certificate to display in your business, and also list your business on our project website as a **contributing sponsor**. Lastly, we offer tax receipts for donations over ten dollars. (Feel free to use the self addressed envelope to send your donation.)

Grande Prairie and District Catholic Schools

On behalf of myself, our class, our school, Craig Kielburger, Iqbal Masih, and all child labourers around the world, I would like to thank you for your anticipated and generous support of our project.

Respectfully,

Mrs. Bonnie Anderson
Gr. 2 Teacher – St. Mary's – Sexsmith

PS: Please enjoy the enclosed letters from the grade two students asking for your help!

PSS: Please consider this a **warm invitation** to our "Labour of Love II Gala Evening" on June 12, 2004 at 7pm at St. Joseph High School Gym. We have a special guest speaker coming from Free the Children, Joe Opatowski, to present to us. Tickets are available at the door by donation or beforehand at St. Patrick Catholic School or St. Mary's in Sexsmith. Come and bring some friends for an awesome evening of information and celebrating our kids' education and accomplishments! ☺

Sample of the business pack we sent to over 60 Businesses! ☺

My Story

ANONYMOUS

We would like to conclude with a final story. This is the story of an individual with remarkable skills and talents. This person has vision, energy, and passion. This person has the power to change the world by reaching out to others—but was awaiting a call. One day, the call came. It didn't take much—there was no epiphany, no cloud opening. All it took was a gentle push.

With a little inspiration, this individual will go on to do great things, contributing to a better world in a unique and personal way. Although these remarkable actions won't make front-page news, they will be permanent etchings in the sands of time, forever remembered by the people who will be touched by them.

The positive energy, born of this one person, will spread like a ripple inspiring others to join a powerful movement to help others. This individual will embody the Movement from *Me to We* and make his or her life more meaningful, fulfilling, and happier than he or she ever dreamt possible.

Who is this person? We hope it will be you.

We don't know how this story will end, but we know how it can continue—with a simple gesture—one first act of giving that will set off a chain of events. We hope that you will gently push another person along this same journey, by now passing this book to someone special in your life.

ISSUE + GIFT = BETTER WORLD
(...AND BETTER YOU!)

Throughout this book, you have read the stories of people who live the *Me to We* philosophy. You have been introduced to individuals like Lindsay Avner, who is taking action to save her own life, that of her mother, and millions of others whom she has never met, by participating in the race to find a cure for breast cancer; the renowned Jane Goodall, who lovingly describes the impanzees she lived with for decades, and who has been rking tirelessly to educate people, especially young people, ut protecting our natural environment; and John Gaither o is spending his senior years volunt

...n can help ...
...on from these pag...
...and a better you.
...the examples presented here ha...
...f you don't have a vision for your action, you have...
...mply by having read these stories, and challeng...
...attuned to the pressing problems and issue th...
...le of the world and will soon find an issue th...
...don't be overwhelmed—keep in mind that f...
...tured here are celebrities, and no...
...world-changers. They are for the most...
...you with one basic element in comm...
...had something to give, and they ga...
...Once you have found your i...
...with your g... and then start...
ce. At the end of this book, you will find...
...n take to help address the social issues...
...h of these stories. You will also be...
stics that reveal the sco...
...end your ...

CHAPTER 12: ...

SEE WHAT THE CONTRIBUTORS HAVE
SAY ABOUT THE ME TO WE PHILOSO...

"At a tender age I discovered that it isn't doing spectacular things that ... you remarkable in the eyes of God, but instead, it is when you lig ... one candle to dispel a little bit of darkness that you are doing som ... tremendous. And if, as a global people, we put all the little bits of g... gether, we will overwhelm the world." —Archbishop Desmon...

"I began to see that nothing I can do will bring me happiness unles... cludes happiness for others. Whenever I suffer, it's really because ... discounted the other. The flip side of that is being genuinely concern ... the other. When this happens, we have a true spontaneous moment ... isfaction, happiness, and joy." —Richar...

"If we think of our life as an effort to fly always just a little bit high ... reach a goal that's just a little bit beyond our reach, we are faced ... question: How high can any of us go by ourselves?" —Dr. Jane G...

"I shared a conviction with my husband that, even in a conflict regio ... as ours, when human needs and aspirations are prioritized in a socie ... society is better able to resist and topple tyrants and extremists. Tha... people have hope and opportunity, they will sacrifice and invest in a ... and peaceful future for their families. And when we invest in young p ... miracles can happen." —Her Majesty Queen Noor of J...

SELF-HELP   0906

ISBN-13: 978-0-7432-9831-5
ISBN-10: 0-7432-9831-4

ple we have met have led us to one shockingly simple con-
sion: being thinner, smarter, richer, faster, or having better
will not make you happy, despite claims to the contrary. In
this book challenges the notion that self-help—worr
retting about yourself all the time.
elf, is the best way to i
ppiness and purpose b
s reverse path led to
re from most books in
ents a complete shift i
and its message. We
a reason: we wanted to
ible.

contributed their ow
apters as examples of
nced in their own lives.
as bedtime heart warr
ial issues discussed in t
or you to use as your sp
orld.

ype of map leads you a
covered and absorbed
fe may not end up a

es, we've sat on panels
spent hours playing
dren from Brazil to Th
ves, as well as meeting
rents, and educators in
n the process we found
least expected to be h
ade another surprisin
out to learn more at
ntered. Upon returni
y invited to speak at
where people gathere
s and peace. We fou
ple selling quick and
e we listened to ther
the more we began to
what we had witnessed in our service
d overseas.

e its inception, Free the Children has grown into an
onal movement of children helping children that has
d the lives of over a million children in more than 35
s. The organization has built over 400 schools to date
ides clean water and medical supplies, and establishes

four, five, eight steps, ten potent questions, and
anteed results. We, on the other hand, of
solution—one habit to being *happy*. If you think
be more steps in a book this size, don't worry; it's
step. We're going to turn self-help on its head!
You may be thinking that we are rather your
ing a book like this. That may be, but being youn
with new ways of looki
ered a simple truth that
nare it with you.
are two brothers from a
who grew up with a lov
involved. In 1995, we fo
on committed to bringin
through this work we
dinary life experiences. W
he world, visiting more th
ave shared simple meals
in the slums of Calcutt
quets with some of the w
at the World Economic
war-torn villages of Sie
people whose limbs we
tias, and at major Unite

With contributions from Richard Gere,
Dr. Jane Goodall, Kim Phuc, Her Majesty Queen Noor,
Archbishop Desmond Tutu, and Oprah Winfrey

Me to We

Finding Meaning in a Material World

CRAIG KIELBURGER
and MARC KIELBURGER

Contents

Preface
Chapter 1: Two Wor
My Story: Kim Phuc
Chapter 2: Our Self-
My Story: Keith Taylor
Chapter 3: Our Self-H
Happiness i
My Story: Tim Lefens
Chapter 4: Me to We (fr
My Story: Archbishop Desn
and Jonathan Wh
Chapter 5: The Roots of S
Chapter 8: Within "We" Is "Me"
My Story: Kathy Buckley
Chapter 9: Helping Other
My Story: Richard Gere
My Story: John Gaith

The Transformation of Monarch Park...

by Sally Hakim

This was not a school I should be going to, I thought. Monarch Park Collegiate had a bad reputation. In Grade 8, I was told that you would be shot, or to make sure you watch who you talk to, because you don't want to be part of the "bad" crowd. I heard that gangs roamed the halls and violence was a daily occurrence.

Monarch was not just a bad choice; it was a bad school. None of my friends were going to be joining me, and that is the end of the world to a Grade 8 student. I chose to go there because it was convenient and my sister had already been attending for three years. She told me it was not as bad as its reputation, but what my friends said I believed much more than anything my sister would say.

After a long summer, the day I dreaded finally arrived and it was the first day of Grade 9. I tagged along with my older sister. This was it—high school. These are supposed to be the best years of my life and I was afraid. I decided that I wasn't going to like it, but I was here, so I might as well make the best of a bad situation.

One of the first things that I noticed was the diversity of this school. I've since learned that MPC has over 70 home languages and students from over 100 countries here. Some students wear traditional Muslim dress. Others wear traditional Western teen clothes. With everyone coming from all corners of the planet there is no majority present. We are a reflection of Toronto.

The Toronto District School Board has a scale of need, looking at schools and the communities they serve. Monarch Park is considered one of the neediest schools in the city. There is nothing that many of our students don't need more of: better housing, better opportunities, more of a sense of hope, more support for single parents, less ghettoization, more hope in every way.

That's what Monarch needs, but what we get is what the community can afford.

I became part of this place. I joined up in a few activities, but I noticed that even though there were things to do, there was no school spirit to speak of. A few individuals joined everything, and most of the other students walked the halls and attended classes, but that was about it. Teachers, although very nice, taught, and students learned, but at Monarch not everyone was engaged.

In my Grade 11 year the student council (a democratic body) elected me to be the school president. I was told about the Free The Children (FTC) organization at a student council meeting, and we decided to buy in. One of the first activities that was arranged was for a speaker, Cheryl, to visit our school and introduce us to Free The Children and what they did.

When Cheryl picked up the mic on the stage we did not know what was going to happen. What did happen was during the speech you could quite literally hear a pin drop. I was sitting backstage not sure how students would react, when, looking out at the audience, I saw that students were hypnotised by her words. The stories she told us—well, we were able to put ourselves into the story.

Students left the auditorium after about an hour. Some left in tears, some angry, but many more got the spark and wanted to know what they could do to make a real change. Classes started but teachers could not teach English or math or science…but rather the discussion was what we could do. Can we, an inner city school in Toronto, really make any difference in the world?

Could we build a school? Some people thought no. Many more, though, said yes. Teachers and students joined forces and began a discussion and were able to openly discuss their viewpoints in an atmosphere of acceptance and of change.

Cheryl from FTC made a snowball and left us to begin to roll it. It was the little snowball that couldn't be stopped. Staff and students became one, together working toward the goal of building a school. Weekly coin collections were started. Food sales were held; clubs began fundraising; classes took on activities.

Soon a global committee was formed and it was decided that Monarch Park Collegiate would get a new focus. It would become a global school. We were mostly pleased with what was happening but we got off late and money was being raised very slowly.

Then tragedy struck. On December 26, 2004, a tsunami hit Southeast Asia and Africa. A group of Monarch students, some staff, and the administration got together on the first day of school back from Christmas holidays, and we realised that something had to be done, and could be done. A plan arose from a meeting: we chose to help by raising funds through food sales, classroom collections, coin drives, bake sales, a raffle for a donated CD player, and door-to-door solicitation in the community.

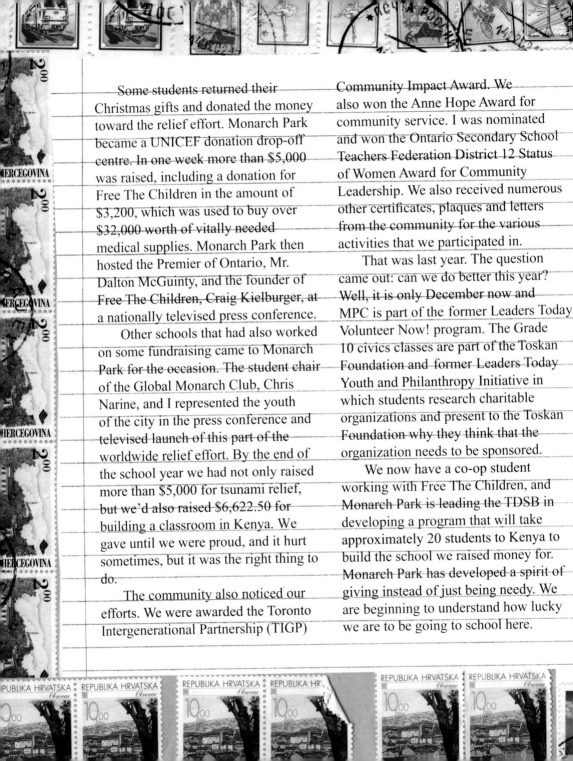

Some students returned their Christmas gifts and donated the money toward the relief effort. Monarch Park became a UNICEF donation drop-off centre. In one week more than $5,000 was raised, including a donation for Free The Children in the amount of $3,200, which was used to buy over $32,000 worth of vitally needed medical supplies. Monarch Park then hosted the Premier of Ontario, Mr. Dalton McGuinty, and the founder of Free The Children, Craig Kielburger, at a nationally televised press conference.

Other schools that had also worked on some fundraising came to Monarch Park for the occasion. The student chair of the Global Monarch Club, Chris Narine, and I represented the youth of the city in the press conference and televised launch of this part of the worldwide relief effort. By the end of the school year we had not only raised more than $5,000 for tsunami relief, but we'd also raised $6,622.50 for building a classroom in Kenya. We gave until we were proud, and it hurt sometimes, but it was the right thing to do.

The community also noticed our efforts. We were awarded the Toronto Intergenerational Partnership (TIGP) Community Impact Award. We also won the Anne Hope Award for community service. I was nominated and won the Ontario Secondary School Teachers Federation District 12 Status of Women Award for Community Leadership. We also received numerous other certificates, plaques and letters from the community for the various activities that we participated in.

That was last year. The question came out: can we do better this year? Well, it is only December now and MPC is part of the former Leaders Today Volunteer Now! program. The Grade 10 civics classes are part of the Toskan Foundation and former Leaders Today Youth and Philanthropy Initiative in which students research charitable organizations and present to the Toskan Foundation why they think that the organization needs to be sponsored.

We now have a co-op student working with Free The Children, and Monarch Park is leading the TDSB in developing a program that will take approximately 20 students to Kenya to build the school we raised money for. Monarch Park has developed a spirit of giving instead of just being needy. We are beginning to understand how lucky we are to be going to school here.

In addition to the Free The Children initiatives, the Toronto Argonauts now sponsor our new breakfast club, providing a hot and nutritious breakfast. There is support for students who need lunches. Monarch is part of the leading edge worldwide ABEL broadband network, allowing students to enjoy city- and worldwide video conferencing.

Next year when I go with my fellow students to Kenya to build a school, we hope that we will be able to keep in contact with home and share our cultural experiences. And the Kenyan students with whom we share this adventure will be able to see and hear our place, our school, the customs and foods and people we work with every day. In the 2006-2007 school year, Monarch Park Collegiate is going to offer the Pre-International Baccalaureate program, a worldwide-recognized high school diploma program, which will be a new level of qualification we can offer our students.

So my life has totally changed during the past three and a half years.

The reputation of Monarch Park Collegiate is still around, but what is nice is that it is changing. Through positive actions and the resulting positive press in the community, people are beginning to recognize what a safe school MPC is and that it is a school that provides students with incredible opportunities to make a difference. MPC opens the doors to opportunity: students decide to walk through.

More importantly, students have begun to realize that the ability to make a positive change is within each of us, regardless of where we come from, what we did in the past, where we live, or our race or nationality. None of our differences really matter. What does matter is that we act—not to help ourselves but to understand that the greatest joy comes from making a difference in the lives of others.

MONARCH PARK
COLLEGIATE

Receved by COSTI
from Kids Can free The Children
And
futures for Youth

120 Health Kits
1 Baby Swing
508 Baby Diapers
73 Stuffed Animals
35 Baby Toys

Received by: Mary Ghawal

Date: June 05, 1999

TO SALVATION ARMY

TOYS → ̶H̶H̶ ̶H̶H̶ ̶H̶H̶ ̶H̶H̶ 111

Adults Clothing → ̶H̶H̶ ̶H̶H̶ ̶H̶H̶ ̶H̶H̶ 1111 1111
boxces ̶H̶H̶ ̶H̶H̶ ̶H̶H̶ ̶H̶H̶ 1111 1111

Children's Clothing ̶H̶H̶1

Infants Clothing

bedding → ̶H̶H̶ 11

Jackets →

Shoes → ̶H̶H̶ 11

hats → 1111

Receipt

Received by the Red Cross at CFB Kingston from Kids Can Free The Children:

1410 Health Kits
160 Bath Kits
270 Baby Kits
206 Stuffed Animals
10,495 Diapers
73 pkgs. Baby Wipes
310 Baby Formula
576 Baby Food
124 Baby Clothing (New)
143 Baby Powder
76 Petroleum Jelly
83 Baby Oil and Lotion
7 Baby Shampoo
36 Nursing Pads
248 Baby Bottles
145 Baby Bibs
1 Roll Diaper Liners (100)
412 Bottles Shampoo
346 Small Bottles Shampoo
6034 Bars Soap
800 Toothbrushes

624 Combs/Brushes
176 Feminine Hygiene Products
130 rolls Toilet Paper
116 Deodorant
133 Medical Supply Items

103 pkgs. Cotton Swabs
226 Misc. Hygiene Products
13 reg. Boxes Kleenex
61 Individual Kleenex
6 pkgs. Cotton Balls
33 Foam Bath/Body Wash/Liquid Soap
40 Puffs & Sponges
12 Towels

Signature:

Name: TERRY YOUNG

May 12, 1999   COSTI

Acknowledging the receipt of 20 Health Kits,
30 Baby Kits and 105 stuffed animals from
Kids Can Free The Children and Futures for Youth.

Heather Jassme.
COSTI Reception Centre.

**INVENTORY FORM
FOR HEALTH & SCHOOL KITS**

DATE RECEIVED: Feb 27, 2001

ITEMS RECEIVED:
Complete school kits: 1
Complete health kits: 3

Incomplete kits:
School kits
Notebooks
Ruler
Scissors
Eraser
Pencils
Pencil Sharpener
Crayons or colour pencils
Coloured construction paper
Tennis ball
Cloth bag

2-1 cloth bag
3-1 comb
3-2 scissors
3-3 bandaids

Health kits
Face towel
Wash cloth
Toothbrush
Toothpaste
Comb
scissors
Band-aids
Bar of soap

Extra Supplies:
1 bottle of shampoo
1 box of napkins
2 soaps

RECEIVED FROM:
NAME OF CONTACT PERSON: Lakeshore Catholic High S
NAME OF THE ORGANIZATION: Lakeshore Catholic High School
ADDRESS: Lakeshore Catholic High School
150 Janet Street
Port Colborne, Ontario L3K 2E7

$50
CAN HELP PURCHASE GOATS OR CHICKENS FOR MILKING/BREEDING

$75
CAN HELP SUPPORT HAND WASHING STATIONS

$100
CAN PURCHASE TEXTBOOKS

$250
CAN HELP BUILD LATRINES AT A SCHOOL

$500
CAN HELP PROVIDING A NUTRITIOUS LUNCH PROGRAM AT A SCHOOL

$1000
CAN HELP SUPPORT BASIC LITERACY AND BUSINESS TRAINING WORKSHOPS FOR ADULTS

$5000
CAN HELP BUILD A CLEAN WATER PROJECT

$8,500
CAN BUILD AND FURNISH A SCHOOL

BUILD A TEAM

Tell others about your issue and ask if they want to help. When people see you are sincere about your area of concern, and hear you say why it is important to help, some of them will want to get involved. These people will be your teammates and you will grow to rely on their support, advice and ideas.

How to get others involved

Motivate Others

Talk to people in your school and community

promote the issue by organizing an exhibit

Put on A Play

Talk to your family and friends

utilize individual talents

SeEK permission to hold an info. presentation at Your sports club.

promote the issue by holding a party

Exercise strong leadership by welcoming everybody's contributions.

distribute flyers

You Children

BUILD A TEAM that is representative of

CALL A MEETING

Once you have a group of people who are interested in your cause, it is time to call a formal meeting. Organizing effective, efficient meetings takes a lot of practice.

Find a Place

Set an Agenda

Have a Definite Purpose

Take Notes

Thank Everyone

Set a Date for the Next Meeting

ꟽ me to we

Me to We began with a simple, basic idea: Helping others makes you happy. Better yet, it also changes the world. The Me to We philosophy challenges everyone to answer the question: What have you done to change the world today?

Me to We Programs

Trips
International Volunteer and Leadership Trips to Kenya, China, India, Ecuador and Arizona

Leadership
Youth Leadership and Volunteer Workshops in North America, including the Take Action Academy

Style
Ethically manufactured, eco-friendly and stylish apparel options for the socially conscious consumer

Speakers
Passionate, riveting stories that will stir hearts and open minds

Music
Fresh, inspiring sounds with a positive message for everyone

Books
A wide collection of captivating books for all ages to challenge, educate and inspire the next generation of change-makers

Events
One-of-a-kind events bringing together thousands of young people, including National We Day

Mobilizers
Bringing the youth and 20-somethings together as social activists that deliver change in their cities

AGRADECEMOS A

Free the Children

POR LA AYUDA BRINDADA
EN LA CONSTRUCCION DE
ESTE LOCAL ESCOLAR
PARA LA EDUCACION DE
NUESTROS HIJOS.
CON EL APOYO DE:
Fundación Chimborazo, Proyecto
Desarrollo de Area. UOCIC.
Chimborazo, Ecuador · 2001

We are grateful to Free The Children for the help offered on
the construction of this academic site for the education of our
children with the help of Chimborazo Foundation.

The question:

"Can You Handle This?"

It was an honest question, not a challenge. A German doctor named Andy ran around. One of the patients had soiled himself. Another patient wet the bed. People served food. People emptied bed pans. The plastic gloves were missing.

"I only have 10 hands, can somebody take this?" Andy handed someone a blanket. Who knows why it needed to go to the laundry.

An American named John oriented me to Mother Teresa's Home for the Destitute and Dying in Calcutta. He warned me in passing: "By the way, the word for 'crap' here is 'shit.' It's not because people are swearing; they just say 'shit.' That's the word: shit. And there's a lot of shit here." He poured water on a soiled toilet seat as he said this. He continued, "When I got here, I was shocked when I heard the nuns say 'shit.' So don't be surprised if you hear them—they say it the most here."

Just a few minutes later John helped change one of the patients. Hans, an elderly German volunteer, told me to put on gloves and get a pair for him. This was all going on ER-room style. I didn't have time to think. As I handed him the gloves he asked me to pull out the sheet from under the patient that John was holding up. I did and started to bunch it to make it easier to carry. As my hand grabbed more of the sheet my hand felt heat. I froze.

Hans looked up at me, shocked and worried. He asked the question: "Oh—can you handle this?" I looked down at the now reeking, stained sheet. I could hardly bear the sight of my hand. Part of me actually wanted to lie. Part of me wanted to say "no." In that moment I searched the room with my eyes.

I looked at Andy, who had come to India to volunteer for three months. He had forgotten to leave. There he was, 14 years later, still going strong. James, a volunteer from Scotland, who was 24 years old, had come to India at age 21 and did not leave. He continues to help in the ward to this day. John, the American, had brought a group of friends to volunteer. He stood there, casually waiting for me to respond as he looked to see what his friends were doing.

Hans had this genuine look of concern on his face. He later told me that it took him three months to muster up the courage to change a soiled sheet. He glanced around the room to anticipate who would need attention next.

Volunteers from all over the world, and India, had come to help in any way they could. I looked at the man who John was still holding up. He had been in an accident. A car had hit him. He also had tuberculosis. He looked me in the eyes and smiled. He was not ashamed. His face was one lending support. No one is to blame for all the help that we need. We all need help.

I nodded.

I smiled.

I grabbed the rest of the sheets and walked to the laundry.

With a slight sense of urgency I patiently searched for a sink in which to wash my gloved hands. As the soap and water did their job, I laughed at myself. "We" are all in this together. We are not above helping anyone. We simply cannot afford to be. But for there to be a "We" in this, the "Me" in all of us must commit. We must come together. There are so many more stains to wash off this tapestry we call humanity. So much need. There is so much comfort and joy that can come from us moving from Me to We.

- Joe Opatowski

"Yesterday, in the school gym, [Nadja] Halilbegovic, 23, American Anitra Sumbry, 9, and Canadian Ed Gillis, 27, began a year-long Embracing Cultures Project tour of 200 North American schools to inspire young people to embrace cultural diversity despite the carnage, in flesh and spirit, of 9/11.

"'It is a walk we must take together. We are models of embracing cultures, and walking together is how we change the world,' the young Bosnian told her audience yesterday.

"The tour is organized by (Kids Can) Free The Children, founded in 1996 by then 12-year-old Canadian Craig Kielburger. The network has more than 100,000 members in 35 countries."

Toronto Star
September 10, 2002

Embracing Diversity

The Embracing Cultures Project will be a meaningful and sustainable addition to the educational development of young people at any school. The benefits of the project include the following:

- Highly talented, experienced youth facilitators, who are young people themselves, will be delivering the presentation.

- A designated Embracing Cultures Project Coordinator will serve as a mentor and facilitator for young people who become active in the project providing support, direction and guidance by phone or e-mail to youth participants.

- A "teacher's guide" will be made available to educators to assist them in making the issues discussed in the presentation applicable to the curriculum of a variety of academic disciplines such as English, Geography, World Issues and Economics.

- Each school will have the opportunity to designate 10-15 of their top youth leaders to receive invaluable intensive one-on-one leadership training, providing them with the tools to become "ambassadors of peace" and help organize the student body to remain involved in the project.

- The presentation will foster a greater feeling of cultural acceptance and harmony within the school, providing the impetus for a more cohesive student body.

- At the end of the presentation, the student body will be given the opportunity to participate in one of 10 meaningful actions they can take to personally become involved in the project.

Uniting Cultures, Building Bridges Web Site:

A unique web-site for students, teachers and parents is a key aspect of this project. The "Uniting Cultures, Building Bridges" site will be youth friendly. Highlights include the following:

An information portal with material on issues relating to cultural diversity, multiculturalism and racism.

"How-to Guides" providing suggestions on how to implement the "10 challenges" in schools and communities.

A place on the site where select pictures and video clips from young people depicting significant cultural traditions can be posted and viewed by their peers.

Valuable resource and curriculum information for teachers and youth leaders!

The Half-A-Million Hands for Peace:

Using paint and canvas, the project will seek to collect "half a million hand prints of young people from North America around the world. This will serve as a powerful symbolic picture of the unity of youth embracing cultural diversity. Every school, community centre and service club visited will be challenged to participate in this aspect of the project. The hands which make up the mural will be put on display at youth gatherings across the nation, at the school and prominent international conference.

Embracing Cultures Project

Message from Craig and Marc Kielburger

Kids Can Free the Children and Leaders Today are organizations that seek to empower young people to become involved in social issues in their communities and around the world. The Embracing Cultures Tour is one of our most exciting projects to date, as it will provide diversity training and peace building skills to over 200,000 youth across North America. We are especially appreciative of Lekha Singh whose support, vision and commitment have made this project a reality.

Young people from around the world responded to the tragic events of September 11th 2001, by volunteering, collecting money and sending artwork, and letters to the children in the United States as well as Afghanistan who were affected by the crisis.

The Embracing Cultures Tour was inspired by the commitment of youth heroes of September 11th who showed the world that young people have a unique opportunity to embrace and celebrate cultural differences as they grow to be active global citizens. Please join us in making this project a success!

Craig Kielburger
Founder, Kids Can Free the Children

Marc Kielburger
Founder, Leaders Today

The Embracing Cultures Project is being organized by two remarkable youth organizations, Kids Can Free the Children and Leaders Today.

- Kids Can Free the Children is the largest network of children helping children in the world, with over 100,000 members in 35 countries.
  - It has built more than 300 primary schools in the developing world, providing education to over 15,000 needy children.
  - The inspirational work of the organization has been featured on Oprah, 60 Minutes, The Today Show, the BBC and many other media.
  - More information can be found at www.freethechildren...

- Leaders Today is a global youth leadership organization that provides leadership training for high schools, universities youth conferences and gatherings.
  - Leaders Today has facilitated leadership training and workshops for the United Nations, The State of the World Forum, Harvard and Stanford Universities, hundreds...

Kids Can Free the Children and Leaders Today are shining examples of the power young people possess to change the world!
- Dr. Jane Goodall

Embracing Differences

Ed Gillis:

Ed Gillis is an expert youth motivational speaker who has trained thousands of young people in leadership skills throughout North America, Asia and Latin America. Ed completed his Masters in International Relations at the Norman Patterson School of Government and was one of a select group of young people chosen to work in the Parliamentary Internship Program hosted by the Canadian House of Commons. He has led international volunteer excursions of young people to India and Nicaragua, building schools and providing for development projects to communities in need.

Nadja Halilbegovich

When Nadja Halilbegovich was three years old, a prolonged war broke out in her place of birth, Sarajevo, Bosnia. During this time, Nadja suffered physical injuries from the shrapnel of a bombshell which landed close to her home. However, within the hard prisoner in the city, Nadja decided not to become the prisoner of her own mind and soul. She became active in music and began performing throughout Sarajevo at schools, hospitals and religious gatherings. She was a spirited writer and began to share her poems and diary entries on national radio. She quickly became known as Sarajevo's "Anne Frank". Luckily, Nadja was able to escape the "Siege of Sarajevo" and flee to the United States to study and live with a host family. She recently graduated from Butler University having completed her studies in vocal performance and theatre. The University honored her with its first ever "Woman of Distinction Award."

Anitra Sumbry

Anitra Sumbry graduated from the Illinois Mathematics & Science Academy in 2001. She is the co-founder and facilitator of IMSA's Leadership Education And Development Training Program as well as the institution's Synergy Project. She is also the Alumni Advisor to IMSA Student Leadership Development. Her volunteer work includes the delivery of medical care and leadership training in Thailand, Kenya and Zimbabwe. She has conducted research, health care, and at the University of Illinois in Chicago in the area of patient education. She currently attends Emory University where she is studying Biology and Political Science.

The Embracing Cultures Project
50 High Oak Trail
Richmond Hill, Ontario
Canada L4E 3L9
www.freethechildren.com
training101@hotmail.com
Tel: 905.760.9382
Fax: 905.760.9157

Celebrating Differences

About the ECP:

The "Embracing Cultures Project" is a program designed to inspire, motivate and challenge young people in middle and high schools across North America to welcome and 'embrace' cultural differences and become peace builders on a local, national and international level.

The rationale for the undertaking is that in our post September 11th world, young people need to be given the opportunity to be pro-active in creating a more just and humane society.

It is the philosophy of the project that cultural diversity and differences among people of various ethnic origins, backgrounds, heritages and traditions should be celebrated in a spirit of friendship and peace.

Project Information:

The program will be administered by a group of remarkable highly gifted youth motivational speakers, who will travel to selected educational institutions and deliver to the student body a 1.5 to 2 hour presentation that will combine multi-media technology, spoken word, music and moving personal stories.

At the end of the presentation, the students will be given the opportunity to become involved in one or more of a select grouping of 10 concrete and sustainable actions they can take in their own lives to "embrace cultures".

The Embracing Cultures Team will remain at the school throughout the day in order to provide intensive leadership training to 10-15 outstanding young leaders from the school in order to equip them with the leadership tools to become "ambassadors of peace".

Morning Session/ Workshops

9-11 am: The Embracing Cultures Team will deliver a unique interactive and educational presentation to the entire student body.

Afternoon Sessions/ Workshop

12-4 pm: The Embracing Cultures Team will be available to provide intensive leadership training to 10-15 selected youth.

Ongoing Support and Sustainability

The participants who wish to be involved in the program will be given on-going support to further the impact.

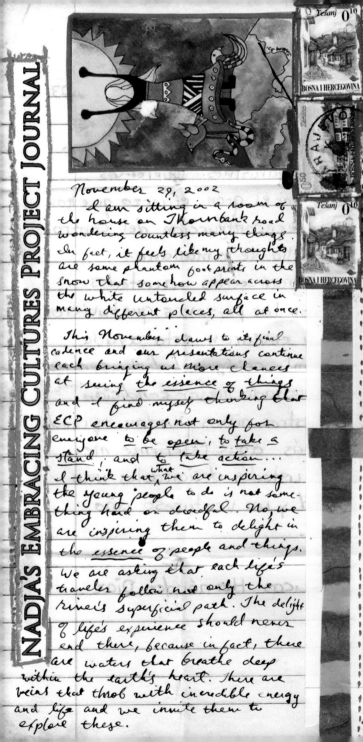

November 29, 2002

I am sitting in a room of the house on Thornbank road wondering countless many things. In fact, it feels like my thoughts are some phantom footprints in the snow that somehow appear across the white untouched surface in many different places, all at once.

This November draws to its final cadence and our presentations continue each bringing us more chances at seeing the _essence_ of things and I find myself thinking that ECP encourages not only for everyone _to_ be _open_, to take _a_ stand, and to take _action_... I think that what we are inspiring the young people to do is not something hard or dreadful. No, we are inspiring them to delight in the _essence_ of people and things. We are asking that each life's traveler follow not only the river's superficial path. The delight of life's experience should never end there, because in fact, there are waters that breathe deep within the earth's heart. There are veins that throb with incredible energy and life and we invite them to explore these.

HAPPY CHILDREN'S

NADJA

1 Put passion and energy into everything you do. LEV3L (Level 3) is not about output, like the volume of your voice or the number of accomplishments you achieve. It is all about input—the energy and passion that you commit to the people in your life, to the issues that are important to you, and to the goals that you seek.

2 Give of yourself. Money and kind words are important and valuable, but they're also easy. Your time and your heart are priceless treasures that only you can give.

3 Be different. Participate and contribute in your own distinctive way. Give to the world your unique talents, style, and ideas. Do NOT be held back by convention or custom (i.e., men don't wear toe nail polish, don't act silly, or dance in public places)—colour the world with the beauty of your individuality and **imagination.**

4 Make people smile and laugh. Smiles and laughter are the most beautiful and powerfully positive sight and sound, respectively, in our world. They are real-life miracles: they magically wash away sadness, conflict, and stress. ¶ All it takes to make someone smile is to smile at them first—a simple, painless, and very powerful way to make someone's day brighter. Develop your sense of humour, and use it often—even in very tense situations. Sing a silly song, make a funny voice, send a funny e-mail. You will live better and longer, and so will everyone else around you.

5 Laugh at yourself. This skill requires self-confidence, humility, and courage—a powerfully selfless act. When you make yourself the focus of ridicule, that burden is relieved of someone else who feels it too regularly. Indirectly, you help others to dwell less on their own inadequacies, and to feel more comfortable with themselves and with you.

6 Be vocal and generous with praise and appreciation. "Great job," "You're awesome," "It's so great having you around," and "I love you" are powerful phrases that make everyone feel good about themselves and about the relationship between you. Use these expressions sincerely and often. If criticism is warranted, be constructive, cautious, and quiet: seek improvement, not blame.

The Eleven Commandments of LEV3L*

* By Ed Gillis, with the inspiration of many special and wonderful people

7 **Understand people.** Know that every person you pass on the street has goals, hopes, and dreams just as you do; everyone you meet has experienced pain, loss, and hardship just as you have; every human being has needs, wants, and emotions of equal value and passion to your own. ¶ Be aware of the reasons why people do what they do—very few people do bad things without cause. The abuser may have been abused; the criminal may have a deep mistrust of the justice in life; the liar may have profound insecurities. The key to healing the world is in showing compassion and true understanding to those who do not fit in, and finding room to include them in our common humanity.

8 **Build yourself up instead of tearing others down.** Search not for the weaknesses of others, but rather seek and develop your strengths, and to know what you can contribute that is special. Competition is not always necessary—realize that we are all playing on the same team with the same goals, hopes, and dreams.

9 **See the beauty in everything.** It isn't hard if you try, it isn't always what you expected, and it is always well worth the effort.

10 **ACT.** Talking and planning only goes so far—changing the world requires concrete action. Lead by example—live your message.

11 **Life exists for two experiences: LOVE and FUN.** What else is life for? Don't work all your life to enjoy a few fleeting moments of happiness. Love and fun should always permeate everything you do. Seek them out: without them, life has little true meaning. With them lies your Power of One. With them, you are unstoppable.

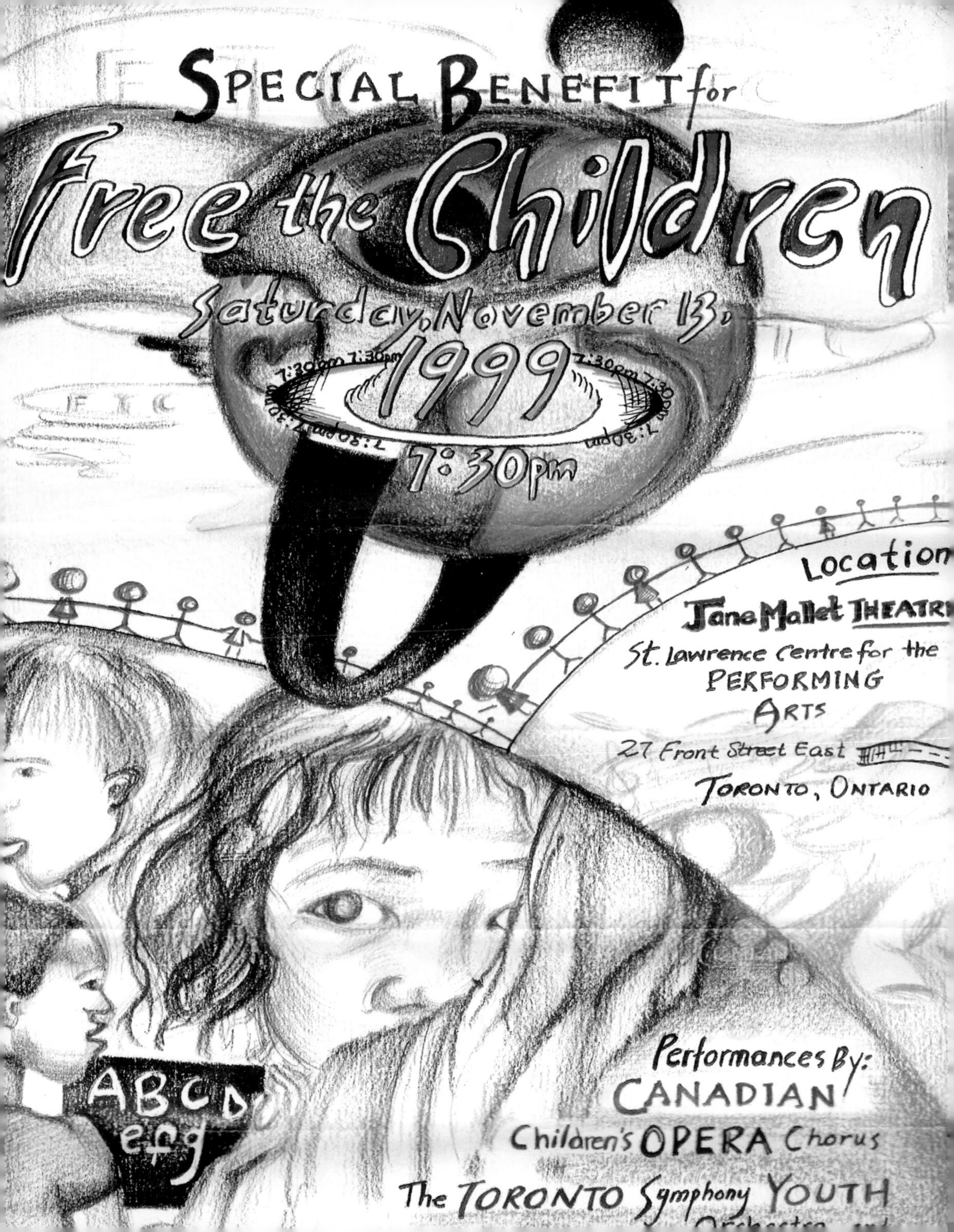
SPECIAL BENEFIT for
Free the Children
Saturday, November 13,
1999
7:30pm
FTC
Location
Jane Mallet THEATR
St. Lawrence Centre for the
PERFORMING
ARTS
27 Front Street East
TORONTO, ONTARIO
ABCD
efg
Performances By:
CANADIAN
Children's OPERA Chorus
The TORONTO Symphony YOUTH

In February 2002, the Free The Children Toronto Chapter organized its first Freedom Jam Benefit Concert in collaboration with the Thornhill Youth Council. The Freedom Jam marked the end of a two-week long War is Not a Game campaign as part of a larger Free The Children Youth Ambassadors for Peace project. The campaign specifically aimed to raise awareness on the issue of war-affected children while spreading an overarching message of peace. The two-week long campaign included war toy collections in various schools across the city and a Peace Quilt project where children from the Toronto community contributed their artistic visions and hopes for peace.

The Freedom Jam aimed to bring together the community for a night of music and dance to celebrate the hard work of all those involved in the two-week long campaign, but most importantly, to continue to raise awareness on war-affected children. People were encouraged to donate their war toys, received information on the campaign, and were given resources to help them learn more about war-affected children. Throughout the night, local young performers showcased their talents—including a five-piece instrumental band, tap-dancing performances to the beats of Michael Jackson's "Man in the Mirror" and "Scream," and a popular Toronto singer-songwriter. The event was hosted by Andrew McCargan, a nationally acclaimed Canadian hip-hop artist, and Jonathan Thiang, a young Toronto activist involved with Free The Children. Members of the Chapter spoke about war-affected children, then shared with the audience a slideshow and stories of children living in some of the world's conflict

The night ended with the audience, performers, and Toronto Chapter members singing along to John Lennon's "Imagine" and then breaking into dance. Since the venue was provided free of charge, thanks entirely to the wonderful support of the Thornhill Youth Council, and sound equipment was donated for the night from Long and McQuade in Toronto, all proceeds from ticket sales ($5 tickets to make them affordable) and donations went to Free The Children's schoolbuilding efforts in Sierra Leone. The country is currently recovering from a bloody civil war that was fuelled by a lucrative diamond trade in which many children were exploited and used as child soldiers. Many of Sierra Leone's children continue to suffer from experiences of gruesome violence, and many of them who had their hands and feet amputated by rebel forces have become poignant reminders of the country's recent conflict.

Perhaps most memorable of the entire event was the incredible spirit of the youth who put this successful night together. All of the organizers and volunteers were youth—and the event reflected this. It was a grassroots initiative where youth painted banners, sewed together the 80-part Peace Quilt to put on display, put together the programs and speaking notes, and performed songs and dance numbers. These efforts resulted in a night that was able to raise funds to contribute to education in Sierra Leone, and through the war-toy drive was able to encourage local youth to recognize that while children in many countries including Canada play war, for many children around the world, war is not a game. It was truly a night that expressed the spirit of Free The Children, a spirit in which young people can use their talents, passion, and leadership to help their peers around the world.

- Janet Cho

War Is Not A Game Campaign

This campaign will raise funds for our Schools For Peace program through sponsors who will donate a set amount for each war toy turned in. Ultimately, the War Is Not a Game campaign* will encourage children in post-conflict zones to turn in their weapons by offering schoolbooks, education and other productive materials in their place. By doing so, war-affected children will be given the opportunity to choose peace over violence and empower themselves with the ability to create a peaceful future for their communities. The War Is Not a Game campaign will help to create a "children-to-children" network whereby youth in conflict and non-conflict regions will be acting in partnership to build a more peaceful world.

- Free The Children

*The War Is Not a Game campaign was a former Free The Children program, offered in partnership with the United Nations.

Artwork by Adam Saltsman

WAR IS NOT A GAME

Children should not be pawns in adult wars...

WAR IS NOT A GAME

Is Not a Game

BEWARE LAND MINES

You Can Make a Difference!

Artwork by Adam Saltsman

101

I think that the most important step in getting involved in activism is to lay a solid foundation. This foundation has to be constructed with knowledge, passion, commitment and energy. Without this groundwork, anything else that is constructed will not be stable and sustainable. Issues such as poverty, hunger, child labour and fair trade are not going to be solved overnight, with one volunteer experience, with one event. They take time and without a strong foundation, a long-term solution can not be found.

For activists, whether they be working locally, nationally or internationally, they have to recognize that the way that they can make the biggest impact is in how they live. After educating yourself about the problem, find solutions that can be implemented in your everyday life and lead by example. It goes along with the old saying "practice what you preach." More people will be willing and wanting to get involved when they don't just hear the words and slogans, or see the signs and numbers, but when they see examples that they can easily get involved with. Activism is not a day job, it's not a "when I feel like it" hobby. It is a lifestyle.

To change the world, you have to be willing to change yourself.

- Danielle Hoegy

STOP CHILD LABOUR

GLOBAL MARCH 1998

WALK FOR CHILD RIGHTS

11 MARCH 1998

SAHID MINAR, CALCUTTA 12 NOON

FREE THE CHILDREN · INDIA · W. BENGAL

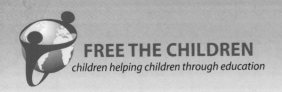

FREE THE CHILDREN
children helping children through education

A celebration of
Free the Children's
achievements.

How Free the Children youth memb[...]
around the world
are making a difference.

How you can get involved
and change the lives of children
on a local, national or international le[...]

FREE THE CHILDREN
children helping children through educa[...]

*an international network of
children helping children*

GLOBAL MARCH

Against Child Labour

FREE THE CHILDREN-INDIA
Vijoynagar, Sodepur Road, Madhyamgram,
West Bengal .. 743 275, INDIA.

*An international
network of children
helping children through
education,
leadership and action*

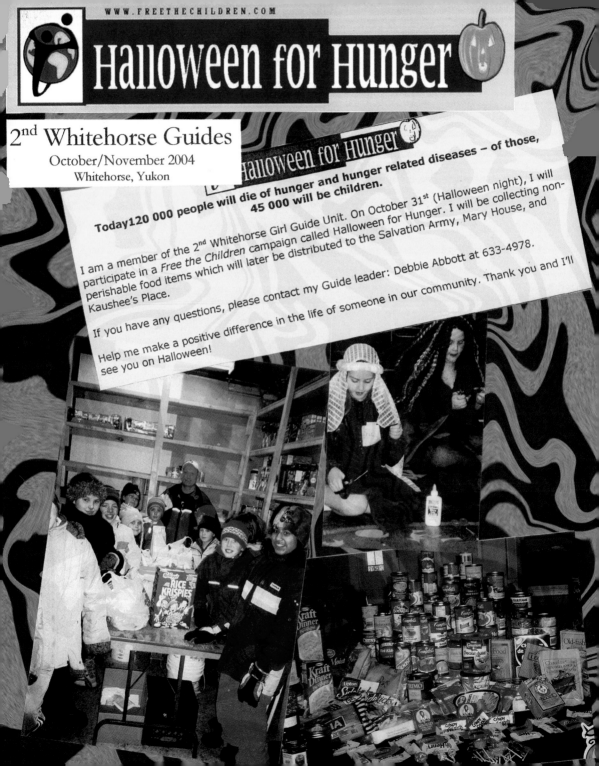

WWW.FREETHECHILDREN.COM

Halloween for Hunger

2nd Whitehorse Guides
October/November 2004
Whitehorse, Yukon

Halloween for Hunger

Today 120 000 people will die of hunger and hunger related diseases – of those, 45 000 will be children.

I am a member of the 2nd Whitehorse Girl Guide Unit. On October 31st (Halloween night), I will participate in a *Free the Children* campaign called Halloween for Hunger. I will be collecting non-perishable food items which will later be distributed to the Salvation Army, Mary House, and Kaushee's Place.

If you have any questions, please contact my Guide leader: Debbie Abbott at 633-4978.

Help me make a positive difference in the life of someone in our community. Thank you and I'll see you on Halloween!

Halloween for Hunger

Halloween4Hunger food drive for Fareshare

A group of local high school students will be collecting canned food donations for Fareshare Food Bank on Halloween night – instead of 'trick or treating.'

It's all part of Halloween 4 Hunger, a project launched by a group of college students in the United States, under the auspices of Sports for Hunger and Free the Children.

Local organizers are Kim Plewes and Kelly Nenniger, both Grade 10 students at Oakville Trafalgar High School.

Last year, students from OTHS collected 2,010 cans of food for Fareshare.

This year, Iroquois Ridge High School students, and youth from Knox Presbyterian Church will join them.

There will also be drop box at Sobeys at Maple Grove Village.

If interested in volunteering or donating, email H4HOakville@hotmail.com.

Halloween for Hunger expands across town

By Craig MacBride
SPECIAL TO THE BEAVER

Halloween is a time of excess; where children gather candy from their neighbours and then gorge on it for the following month.

Kim Plewes is trying to change that though. As children eat candy to their delight, there are people in the community who are having a hard time getting any food at all.

That's why the Grade 12 student brought the international campaign Halloween for Hunger to Oakville in 2000, and it's why she's increasing her efforts this year by taking the program beyond the walls of her own school, Oakville Trafalgar High School.

The program involves students taking part in the ultimate Halloween ritual of trick-or-treating, but instead of holding their bags open for candy, they ask for non-perishable food items that will, once collected, be taken to the Fareshare food bank in Oakville.

Residents in the areas where non-perishable food will be collected are given notice ahead of time, as students taking part will be handing out flyers to the houses where they intend to trick-or-treat. Plewes and the group she has organized have also planned their routes so that they don't overlap. With 25 groups taking part, they already have a lot of Oakville covered.

Two years ago, the last time Plewes organized the event, the Halloween for Hunger gang collected 3,200 cans of food to donate to the foodbank.

"My goal is to beat what we've done in the previous years," said Plewes.

With Iroquois Ridge High School, White Oaks Secondary School, T.A. Blakelock High School and St. Thomas Aquinas all taking part this year, beating those previous numbers should be achievable.

She added, "I do it every year because it's a great way to have fun, spend time with your friends and help your community."

For more information about Halloween for Hunger, or to learn how to take part, email Plewes at oakvilleh4h@hotmail.com.

Teens want food, not treats

A group of local teens, calling themselves Halloween for Hunger (H4H), will be collecting canned and non-perishable food donations for Fareshare Food Bank, instead of trick or treating.

The teens represent Oakville Trafalgar High School (OTHS), Knox Presbyterian Church, and Fareshare Food Bank. Donation boxes have been placed at Knox Church and at OTHS.

The OTHS student council is H4H all food collected at their Haunted House – admission is a can of food.

Flyers are currently being distributed announcing the group's plans to go knocking door to door on Halloween to collect food donations.

The group will present the food to Fareshare about a week after Halloween.

For more information, call Kim Plewes at 849-1623, or send email to kim_ftc@hotmail.com.

kids can
FREE THE CHILDREN

Fundraising Made Easy

Qualities of a Great Fundraiser
- Visionary
- Able and willing to talk straight
- A good listener
- Open and receptive
- Unafraid and bold
- Recognizes that it is a privilege to ask people for money
- Capacity and commitment to bring joy and fun to the job
- Tough, resilient, clear and strong
- Forthcoming and sensitive

The Keys to Fundraising Money
- Ask, ask, ask
- Strategic terminology:
  "Your contribution will help us achieve..."
  "Other individuals who are currently supporting us include..."
  "We are really passionate about this issue because..."
  "I hope we can count on your support!"

Ask the Community for Help!
- Business donations (local and corporate)
- Parents/relatives
- Service clubs (Rotary International, Lions Club...)
- In-kind donations
- Schools and school boards
- Contests and competitions

Fundraising at Your School
- BBQs/pizza lunches
- Fashion shows
- Booth at community events
- Theatre events
- Talent nights
- Auctions/raffles
- Celebrity events

While in Grade 5, my daughter helped to bring a Me to We event to her school and community. She was so inspired by what she learned and the great experience she had, she committed herself to raise money to build a school. In four months she raised $3,000 and inspired a community.

From this, the following year we organized and went on a humanitarian trip to Costa Rica. My daughter said that raising the money was great, but she wanted to go and do the work! This year (she is now 12) she heard a Me to We speaker at her school and has again committed herself to going to a developing country to work.

- Sandra Richardson

Make a Pla

Making a plan of action is often one of the most exciting steps of leadership. Your action plan will be your compass and guide to making a difference. Now brainstorm. Come up with creative, crazy and fun ideas and ways to positively affect your issue.

1. **Define Your Goal: What do you want to accomplish?**

2. **List people who will help you and those who might oppose your cause.**

3. **Develop a strategy.**

4. **Create a message and a logo for your cause.**

5. **Map your actions on a calendar.**

6. **Plan media and education.**

7. **Create a budget.**

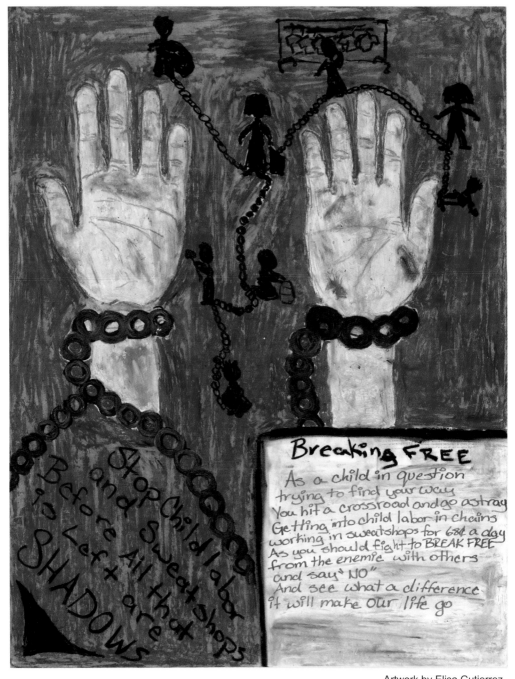

Breaking FREE

As a child in question
trying to find your way
You hit a crossroad and go astray
Getting into child labor in chains
working in sweatshops for 68¢ a day
As you should fight to BREAK FREE
from the enemie with others
and say "NO"
And see what a difference
it will make our life go

Stop Child labor and sweatshops Before All that is Left are not SHADOWS

Artwork by Elisa Gutierrez

Kids Can Free The Children
Child Soldiers Project Proposal
September 22, 2001

Summary

At the Free The Children conference in August 2001, a motion was passed to create Free The Children chapters in universities, including the University of Toronto (U of T). Sheena Kamal and Heather John have undertaken the overseeing of the chapter at U of T for the 2001-2002 school year, and have begun to design the first project for the group to undertake. This project will fall under the realm of the Children In Armed Conflict Project and would include collecting shoes for children in war-torn countries, a major education campaign on and around the U of T campus, and possibly a fundraising component. These goals will be obtained by creating a partnership with the Bata Shoe Museum and exhibiting a display in their lobby for two weeks, and a publicized lecture event at U of T where several speakers, children and adults, would address the topic of child soldiers. Participants would then be presented with several actions they could take to help with the problem of child soldiers.

- Create an exhibit in the Bata Shoe Museum, which is located at Bloor Street and St. George Street, directly adjacent to the U of T campus. This exhibit would last for possibly two weeks and would include information about child soldiers, publicize the upcoming lecture at the university, and could ask for cash donations to help build schools. Ideally, several evenings a week a child (under 18) member of Free The Children would man the booth and explain the project to people. This person could also be joined by an over-18 representative from U of T. The main objective is to collect shoes, so it is a possibility, for example, to have Bata, for each $5 that is donated by an individual, to match that by donating one pair of children's shoes to the cause.
- A large event in a theatre on U of T campus occurring once the booth has finished its time in the museum. Admission would be a pair of shoes, or $5. Speakers would include, tentatively, a speech by a child Free The Children member, a lecture by a professor deeply involved in the issue of child soldiers (for example, Jonathan White), a representative from Free The Children's partner organization in Sierra Leone, ideally a child, who can speak firsthand about the effects of the war. Interspersed among the speakers would be Capoeira, a Brazilian fighting-dance team, and a short play on child soldiers written and performed by kids in Free The Children, possibly with the help of U of T drama students.
- While people are waiting to go into the event, Free The Children reps (under 18) could walk around, each with a different sign saying who they are and a child soldier's story to tell as if it were their own.
- In order to raise extra money for schoolbuilding, there could be a raffle at the event with prizes donated from local sponsors.
- All people at the event will be given suggestions on ways that they can get involved with the issue of child soldiers, such as signing a petition. Especially for students, one of the possibilities would be participating in the day of silence.

One of my biggest pushes to really committing myself to activism came when I realized that I was not the only person in the world who wanted to make a difference, but that there is an **army of youth** all around the world that is committed to making our world a more fair, equal, happy place for all.

- Danielle Hoegy

Artwork by A. Hornig

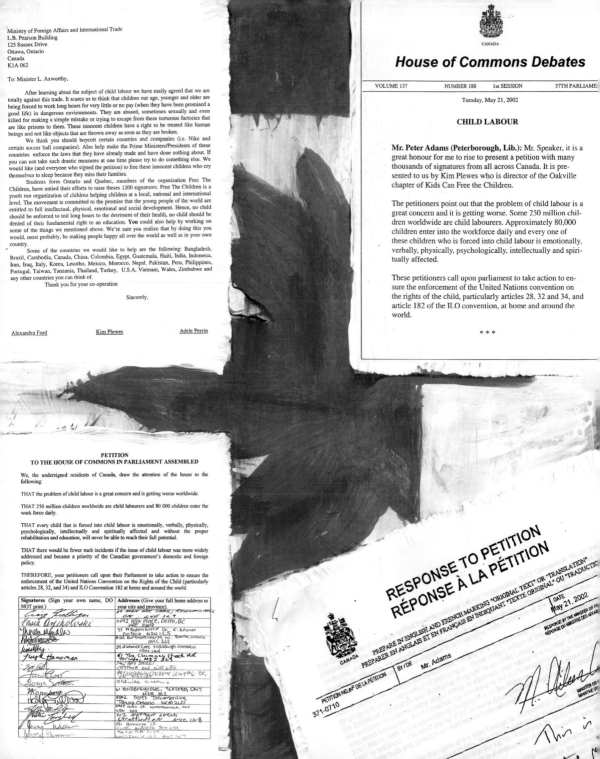

Ministry of Foreign Affairs and International Trade
L.B. Pearson Building
125 Sussex Drive
Ottawa, Ontario
Canada
K1A 0G2

To: Minister L. Axworthy,

After learning about the subject of child labour we have easily agreed that we are totally against this trade. It scares us to think that children our age, younger and older are being forced to work long hours for very little or no pay (when they have been promised a good life) in dangerous environments. They are abused, sometimes sexually and even killed for making a simple mistake or trying to escape from these torturous factories that are like prisons to them. These innocent children have a right to be treated like human beings and not like objects that are thrown away as soon as they are broken.

We think you should boycott certain countries and companies (i.e. Nike and certain soccer ball companies). Also help make the Prime Ministers/Presidents of these countries enforce the laws that they have already made and have done nothing about. If you can not take such drastic measures at one time please try to do something else. We would like (and everyone who signed the petition) to free these innocent children who cry themselves to sleep because they miss their families.

Students form Ontario and Quebec, members of the organization Free The Children, have untied their efforts to raise theses 1200 signatures. Free The Children is a youth run organization of children helping children at a local, national and international level. The movement is committed to the promise that the young people of the world are entitled to full intellectual, physical, emotional and social development. Hence, no child should be enforced to toil long hours to the detriment of their health, no child should be denied of their fundamental right to an education. You could also help by working on some of the things we mentioned above. We're sure you realize that by doing this you would, most probably, be making people happy all over the world as well as in your own country.

Some of the countries we would like to help are the following: Bangladesh, Brazil, Cambodia, Canada, China, Colombia, Egypt, Guatemala, Haiti, India, Indonesia, Iran, Iraq, Italy, Korea, Lesotho, Mexico, Morocco, Nepal, Pakistan, Peru, Philippines, Portugal, Taiwan, Tanzania, Thailand, Turkey, U.S.A, Vietnam, Wales, Zimbabwe and any other countries you can think of.

Thank you for your co-operation

Sincerely,

Alexandra Ford   Kim Plewes   Adele Perrin

Tuesday, May 21, 2002

CHILD LABOUR

Mr. Peter Adams (Peterborough, Lib.): Mr. Speaker, it is a great honour for me to rise to present a petition with many thousands of signatures from all across Canada. It is presented to us by Kim Plewes who is director of the Oakville chapter of Kids Can Free the Children.

The petitioners point out that the problem of child labour is a great concern and it is getting worse. Some 250 million children worldwide are child labourers. Approximately 80,000 children enter into the workforce daily and every one of these children who is forced into child labour is emotionally, verbally, physically, psychologically, intellectually and spiritually affected.

These petitioners call upon parliament to take action to ensure the enforcement of the United Nations convention on the rights of the child, particularly articles 28, 32 and 34, and article 182 of the ILO convention, at home and around the world.

* * *

PETITION
TO THE HOUSE OF COMMONS IN PARLIAMENT ASSEMBLED

We, the undersigned residents of Canada, draw the attention of the house to the following:

THAT the problem of child labour is a great concern and is getting worse worldwide.

THAT 250 million children worldwide are child labourers and 80 000 children enter the work force daily.

THAT every child that is forced into child labour is emotionally, verbally, physically, psychologically, intellectually and spiritually affected and without the proper rehabilitation and education, will never be able to reach their full potential.

THAT there would be fewer such incidents if the issue of child labour was more widely addressed and became a priority of the Canadian government's domestic and foreign policy.

THEREFORE, your petitioners call upon their Parliament to take action to ensure the enforcement of the United Nations Convention on the Rights of the Child (particularly articles 28, 32, and 34) and ILO Convention 182 at home and around the world.

Signatures (Sign your own name, DO NOT print.)	Addresses (Give your full home address or your city and province).

RESPONSE TO PETITION
RÉPONSE À LA PÉTITION

PREPARE IN ENGLISH AND FRENCH MARKING "ORIGINAL TEXT" OR "TRANSLATION"
PRÉPARER EN ANGLAIS ET EN FRANÇAIS EN INDIQUANT "TEXTE ORIGINAL" OU "TRADUC

DATE May 21, 2002

PETITION NO.º DE LA PÉTITION 371-0710   BY/DE Mr. Adams

Sadly, history tends to forget that young people have always been at the forefront of the world's great social justice movements. When the idea of these movements was first born, when victory was far from assured and change seemed impossible, it was young people who dreamed of a better world and who set themselves to achieving that goal. Students, younger than you or me, bore the brunt of the water cannons and the attack dogs during the bus boycotts and freedom rides for civil rights. During the salt marches for independence, Indian children were arrested by the hundreds. Young people were shot and killed as they protested against apartheid in South Africa.

Let me ask you now. What is our social justice movement? What is the struggle to be fought for in our time? By our generation?

Some adults say that the age of great movements is dead, that young people today are too comfortable, even apathetic. Some adults say that low voter turnout of youth shows we have forgotten the sacrifices of Susan B. Anthony, a woman who fought to ensure that all people—men and women both—had the right to cast a ballot. Some adults say that the race-based violence in our schools shows we have forgotten the struggles of Booker T. Washington and Dr. King to ensure that people are judged not by the color of their skin, but by the content of their character. Some adults say that because the youth channel of choice is MTV instead of the news, we have forgotten the example of Mother Teresa to never ignore the sufferings of others.

To these adults, I say you are wrong.

Some young people say there is nothing left to fight for—that all battles have been won. Some young people say that there is no movement to join. Where are the protests, the boycotts, the underground newspapers? Are they simply part of the "flower power" of the past? Some young people say that even if they raise their voice, it's futile, it's pointless, it's wasted—we can't make a difference. We have to wait until we are older, until we graduate from high school, go to college or university, get a job, gain money and a position of influence—only then can we make a positive change in the world.

To these youth, I say that you, too, are wrong.

This is a time for action. We are not apathetic! There is much left to fight for! In our work, we have a slogan: "We are the generation that we have been waiting for!" And this means that we are not simply the leaders of tomorrow. We are called to be the leaders of today!

- Craig Kielburger, at the 2005 Community of Christ International Peace Award Ceremony

Children do not need a Job!

They need love, education and playtime

love is the sunlight education is the good soil play time is the water

Like a tree

Artwork by Coklar Irfan

Children have the right to be children.

Artwork by Kaitlin Boyle

The children of All Saints Elementary School raised $5,430 to build a school in Pandiassou, Haiti, by selling freezies, collecting pennies and selling their toys at a garage sale.

Artwork by Martha Escobar

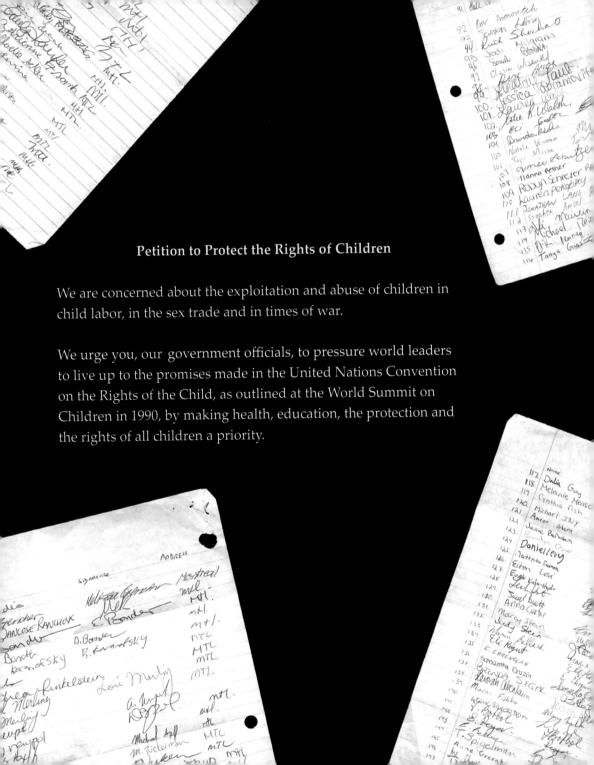

Petition to Protect the Rights of Children

We are concerned about the exploitation and abuse of children in child labor, in the sex trade and in times of war.

We urge you, our government officials, to pressure world leaders to live up to the promises made in the United Nations Convention on the Rights of the Child, as outlined at the World Summit on Children in 1990, by making health, education, the protection and the rights of all children a priority.

We are concerned about the exploitation and abuse of children
in child labour, in the sex trade, and in times of war.

We urge you , our government officials, to pressure world
leaders as live up to the promises made in the United Nations
Convention on the Rights of the Child, as outlined at the
World Summit on Children in 1990,by making health,education,
the protection and the rights of all children a priority.

Name	Signature	Address

We are here to visit a school built by Free The Children, an international organization dedicated to ending child exploitation and servitude through, among other initiatives, the promotion of child education. One of their strongest projects is their schoolbuilding campaign. I am traveling with Free The Children's partner organization, Me to We, dedicated to empowering and educating young people throughout the world to become leaders through international volunteer opportunities and leadership training. As a participant in Summer Leadership Ecuador, I am traveling throughout the Chimbarazzo region for two weeks, exploring several rural communities as well as Quito, the capital city.

A Spanish novice, I'm never sure what my greeters are saying. But it doesn't matter. Engulfed in hugs and handshakes from the children of Llilla, I am part of the family, connected not by language but by the bonds of community. I am not a stranger, but a distant cousin from America.

- Amanda Erickson

Kids Can Free The Children
Suite 300
7368 Yonge Street
Thornhill, Ontario
L4J 8H9 Canada

Dear Sir or Madam:

In school we are reading about child labor and I feel that there shouldn't be child labor. I feel that children under the age of sixteen should not have to work in places that can harm them physically or mentally. I want to know what I can do to help stop child labor and keep the world free of child labor. Write back.

Sincerely,
Rebecca Glatfelter
Rebecca Glatfelter

Kids Can Free The Children
Suite 300
7368 Yonge Street
Thornhill, Ontario
L4J 8H9 Canada

Dear Manager,
I am writing to you, because I feel sad for the young and older children in labor. A lot of these kids are working very hard and get sick. Some kids are very young and might die with to much work. All I'm saying is get rid of child labor! When some want they should, but if they don't want to work they shouldn't. I'll be happy if you do.

Thomas
Matt

Kids can free the children
Suite 300
7368 yonge stree
Thornhill, Ontario
L4J 8H9 Canada

Dear Sir sor Madam:

I think child labor is a bad ide I hop that we wi stop it!!! will you jorn my?

Sincere

Take Action and Then Review

Taking action is key to turning your ideas into reality. If you are planning a Human Rights Awareness Day, make certain you follow through on your idea. If you are collecting school and health kits for children in developing countries, do your very best to collect as many kits as you can. It is actions that create real and lasting change in the world.

Once you have acted, it is important to review and evaluate each action so that you can become more effective. You may want to look at the planning, the actions taken, the media, the people involved and the results.

Here are some questions you may want to ask yourself. Write down your answers to the questions and keep them in a file so that they can be reviewed when you start the next project.

Although you may find it dificult to criticize your work, constructive criticism can be very valuable. Be proud of your achievements.

Enjoy one another's company and try to think of ways to do even better next time.

- What were the positive aspects of the project? Negative?
- How can we improve our project and actions next time?
- How well did we work as a team?
- What new areas of responsibility do we need to add to our team next time?
- Did the team members encounter any major obstacles?
- Did the team have enough or too much adult guidance and support?
- What did each of us learn form this project?
- What might each of us do differently next time?

Esta escuela ha sido construida con la ayuda de
OPRAH'S ANGEL NETWORK & FTC SCHOOLS
"Hua Hua alli causa Charina" "Kids Can Free The Children"
Chañag Piñañan – oct. 2001

This school has been built with the help of
Oprah's Angel Network and FTC Schools.

Our first full day at the Maasai Mara was spent at the work site, digging a trench to lay the foundation of the new school. After three days of digging, we learned that it takes the Kenyan workers one and a half days to dig a trench with three of them...there were 30 of us.

Our first Monday at the Mara was likely the most exciting for most of us. We were finally going to start teaching the children of a nearby school, Emori Joi. We would be teaching them English, math, and science. Naturally, with my lack of skills in the latter two, I taught English.

Every morning, when we arrived at the school, the 300 or so children would make their way, like a stampede, to wrap their arms around us and make us feel welcome. Nothing in my life will ever top the feeling of joy I got from greeting those children every morning.

We spent the majority of the month in a daily routine. We would be up by 7 a.m. and at school by 8 a.m. We would teach until 12:30 p.m. and then head back to camp for lunch. After lunch, we would have a Swahili lesson and then head off to the work site. We would stay at the work site till approximately 6 or 7 p.m. each night.

- Crystal Melo

Kids Can Free The Children
Suite 300
7368 Yonge Street
Thornhill, Ontario
L4J8H9 Canada

Dear Sir or Madam:

Hello, my name is Chris House and I am concerned about child labor. Our fifth grade class at Orchard Grove Elementary School just finished reading about an article in the Time For Kids Magazine regarding kids in who work in banana plantations in Ecuador. They have to climb trees four times their height, work with heavy and extremely sharp knifes and dangerous chemicals. If we stop buying their products they may let the children go and increase adult wages to make them return to work. We also read about the Mill Children from the 1800's and if we could fix that problem over 200 years ago, then maybe we can fix this too. I have attached the article to this letter. Please write back.

Concerned Citizen,

Chris House
Chris House

... The following morning we awoke to the soon-to-become-familiar sound of a loud cow bell being rung.

We ate breakfast quickly, hopped in the lorry, and after about a 10-minute drive, we were at the construction site we soon learned was to become a new school for the local community once we were through with it. The project was in its infancy. One building already had its walls up but no roof. They planned on constructing two more buildings. That day we began digging the foundation trenches of each of these two buildings. The progress was staggering as we exhausted ourselves with pickaxes, shovels and often our bare hands. We worked hard until about 5 p.m. when, exhausted and frustrated with our fleeting attempts at digging the 4-foot trench, we all wandered over the area where a group of children had gathered to watch us. This was to become an afternoon ritual. We played with the little kids. We taught them the song "Boom Chicka Boom," which they immediately embraced. We departed from the construction site... Sleep that night came quickly to all of us after retiring soon after our later dinner.

— Peter Stewart

The Boy and His Chickens

My name is Colin. I'm 12 years old. I live in Santa Barbara, California, with my mom, my sister Ashley, my brother Christopher, my grandparents and my dog Coco. I recently learned about Free The Children and wanted to help. I get an allowance every week, so I saved $20 and sent it to Craig. After I saw the video on how Free The Children helps change the lives of children all over the world I wanted to find a way to raise money so I could make a contribution every month. I talked to my grandparents about how lucky I felt that I had so many blessings in my life and wanted to make sure other children could have the same opportunities as me. They suggested we buy baby chicks. They would grow up to be chickens, and I could sell the eggs. When we brought the chickens home I helped grandpa make the chicken coop. They were very young at first, and we had to keep them in the kitchen under lamps so they would stay warm. They

grew very quickly and soon they were jumping out of their boxes. I gave all 14 of them names. I talked to friends and teachers about my project and they agreed to buy eggs from me. I guess I have learned that no matter how old you are you can always find a way to help make a difference in someone else's life. I'm happy to know that somewhere in the world another kid is smiling because I care about them.

Photos courtesy of Holly Lepere

ETHIOPIA

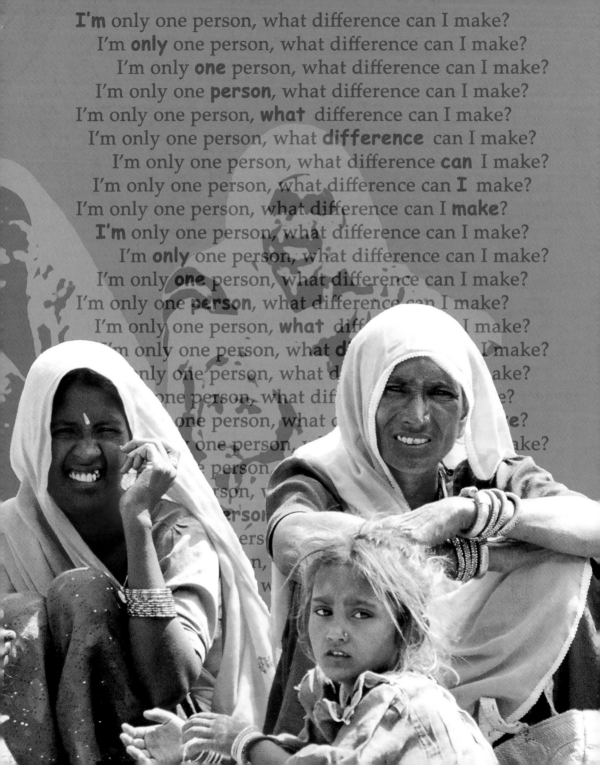

I'm only one person, what difference can I make?
I'm **only** one person, what difference can I make?
I'm only **one** person, what difference can I make?
I'm only one **person**, what difference can I make?
I'm only one person, **what** difference can I make?
I'm only one person, what **difference** can I make?
I'm only one person, what difference **can** I make?
I'm only one person, what difference can **I** make?
I'm only one person, what difference can I **make**?
I'm only one person, what difference can I make?
I'm **only** one person, what difference can I make?
I'm only **one** person, what difference can I make?
I'm only one **person**, what difference can I make?
I'm only one person, **what** difference can I make?
I'm only one person, what d...I make?
...nly one person, what d...ake?
...one person, what dif...e?
...one person, what d...e?
...one person, ...ake?
...person,
...rson,
...erso...
...ers...
...n,
...w

"It was the first time I had ever been involved in a political demonstration..."

"I looked over my shoulder at the people marching behind me. I was tremendously moved by the mothers in their saris, holding their signs for all to see. Many had come from villages outside Calcutta; many had lost children in the explosions at the fireworks factories. It took tremendous courage to march in protest against the factory owners, often the only employers in their small villages. They had made enemies among their own people for doing so. I was overwhelmed by the strength of their conviction, and that of the children who marched along at their sides. I felt it was not my place to lead; they should be the people in front. I took up a position near the rear of the line.

"One mother on the march had been cooking chapattis when the force of an explosion at the local fireworks factory rocked her tiny home. She collapsed in shock, and remained unconscious for 12 hours. The blast had killed both her boys. Their bodies were unrecognizable..."

- Craig Kielburger
Free The Children

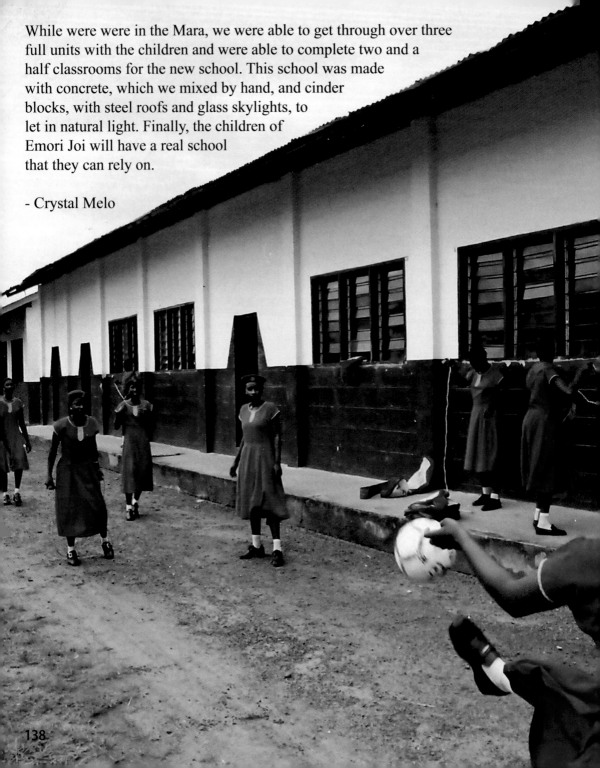

While were were in the Mara, we were able to get through over three full units with the children and were able to complete two and a half classrooms for the new school. This school was made with concrete, which we mixed by hand, and cinder blocks, with steel roofs and glass skylights, to let in natural light. Finally, the children of Emori Joi will have a real school that they can rely on.

- Crystal Melo

December 17, 2002

Dear Free the Children,

We are Mrs. Dell's 6th grade class from Waiau Elementary School in Hawaii. We were inspired by the spectacular presentation you gave us at our school. After the presentation, we felt touched and heart warmed so we wanted to help. We decided to raise 200 dollars to buy a cow for the Alternative Income Project in India. We earned it by doing chores for our families in exchange for money. We also brought in our extra coins. We hope to bring happiness to the family who receives the cow. Please make sure the child in the family that receives the cow has a good education instead of working hard all day.

We are also enclosing 10 dollars extra for a health kit. Can we please have a picture of the family who receives our cow? We are enclosing a self addressed, stamped envelope. We are also enclosing a picture of our class for the family.

Thank you for inspiring us to share our Aloha (love) with people we don't know.

Matt Yamashita

Mahalo nui loa,
(thank you very much)
Mrs. Dell's class

Derek Alvaros
Mike
Nick R
Journey C.E.B. Fernandez
Healing
Michi
Nicholas I.
Rylan Murakami
Keani L. Francis
Erlynn Katayama
Alexis Vega
Oley

print and mail us this form.)

nce for a better life.

☐ Monthly Giving   ☐ Annual Giving

yearly
heir

t of Pledge: $ 210.11   ☑ USD   ☐ CAD

of Payment: We want our money to purchase
                     a cow for the alternative
                     income program
☐ heque/Money Order   ☐ Visa   ☐ MasterCard

s. Dell's sixth Grade Class

ress:
                                    Province/State
Postal Code/Zip:
Work Phone:
Email:
tion: Waiau   Grade (if in school): 6
       Elementary
r Name: Signature:
Card Number: Expiry:
(Make your donation in honor or in memory of someone)
Name of Person:

http://www.freethechildren.org/main/donationform.htm   1/15/03

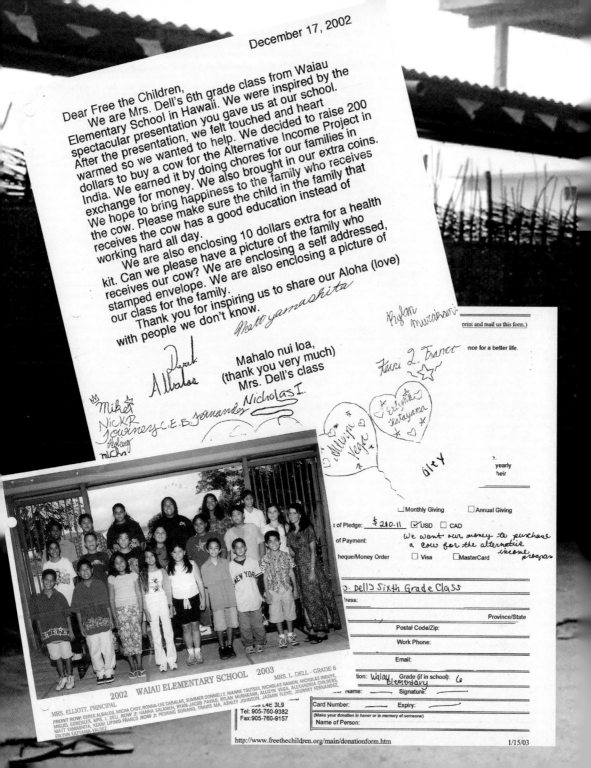

2002   WAIAU ELEMENTARY SCHOOL   2003   MRS. L. DELL - GRADE 6

MRS. ELLIOTT, PRINCIPAL
FRONT ROW: DEREK ALBALOS, MICHA CHUY, RONNA-LEE CABALAR, SUMMER DONNELLY, RIANNE TSUTSUI, NICHOLAS RAMON, NICHOLAS INOUYE,
MIGUEL GONZALES, MRS. L. DELL ROW 2: HANNA SALAMEH, RYAN-JACOB PAVAO, RYLAN MURAKAMI, ALLISYN VEGA, ALEXANDRIA CHILDERS,
MATT YAMASHITA, KEANI LIPINID-FRANCO ROW 3: PEDRING SORIANO, TRAVIS MA, ASHLEY JOHNSON, JASMIN FLOYD, JOURNEY FERNANDEZ,
ERLYNN KATAYAMA, VALDEZ
Tel: 905-760-9382
Fax:905-760-9157
L4E 3L9

Calcium Primary School's
Make a Difference Day 2003

Name Kaitlyn   Age 6

I donated $.50 to help buy a cow for a family in India. The money will go to the Free the Children organization. Now some children can go to school instead of work.

I earned the money by: giving up my
ice cream money.

Draw or write about what you have learned about being a Calcium Peacemaker through this year's project.

Thank you for choosing to make a positive difference in this world!

Calcium Primary School's
Make a Difference Day 2003

Name Ty Dre Daniels   Age 8

I donated $10.00 to help buy a cow for a family in India. The money will go to the Free the Children organization. Now some children can go to school instead of work.

I earned the money by:
Sorting recycable items

Draw or write about what you have learned about being a Calcium Peacemaker through this year's project.

SHARING

Thank you for choosing to make a positive difference in this world!

Calcium Primary School's
Make a Difference Day 2003

Name Kasay Fuller   Age

I donated 2 to help buy a cow for a family in The money will go to the Free the Children organizat Now some children can go to school instead of work.

I earned the money by:
Doing chores for My
GrandMa.

Draw or write about what you have learned about be Calcium Peacemaker through this year's project.

if you put money in the wishi
you will
buy a
cow and free

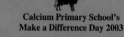

Calcium Primary School's
Make a Difference Day 2003

Name Hannah Overmyer 1-D   Age 6

I donated $5.00 to help buy a cow for a family in India. The money will go to the Free the Children organization. Now some children can go to school instead of work.

I earned the money by:
Helping my mom and dad with my new twin sisters.
I clean my room and around the house.

Draw or write about what you have learned about being a Calcium Peacemaker through this year's project.

Thank you for choosing to make a positive difference in this world!

Calcium Primary School's
Make a Difference Day 2003

Name Asia Small   Age 5y-old

I donated $1.02a to help buy a cow for a family in India. The money will go to the Free the Children organization. Now some children can go to school instead of work.

I earned the money by: helping my mom
with my baby sister.

Draw or write about what you have learned about being a Calcium Peacemaker through this year's project.

I learned to help

Asia — Baby Madison

Thank you for choosing to make a positive difference in this world!

Calcium Primary School's
Make a Difference Day 2003

Name Devon   Age

I donated $5 to help buy a cow for a family in The money will go to the Free the Children organizat Now some children can go to school instead of work.

I earned the money by:
doing chores

Draw or write about what you have learned about be Calcium Peacemaker through this year's project.

cow

Thank you for choosing to make a positive difference in this

Calcium Primary School's
Make a Difference Day 2003

Name Madisson Foster   Age 6

I donated $1 to help buy a cow for a family in India. The money will go to the Free the Children organization. Now some children can go to school instead of work.

I earned the money by: cleaned my
room

Draw or write about what you have learned about being a Calcium Peacemaker through this year's project.

Helping People

Calcium Primary School's
Make a Difference Day 2003

Name Rachel Jaks   Age 7

I donated 5.00 to help buy a cow for a family in India. The money will go to the Free he Children organization. Now some children can go to school instead of work.

I earned the money by: unloading the dishwasher for
2 weeks

Draw or write about what you have learned about being a Calcium Peacemaker through this year's project.

I learned you have
to work really

Calcium Primary School's
Make a Difference Day 2003

Name Rolani Mann   Age 7

I donated 2.00 to help buy a cow for a family in India. The money will go to the Free the Children organization. Now some children can go to school instead of work.

I earned the money by: my Birthday parties and doing
art sale too.

Draw or write about what you have learned about being a Calcium Peacemaker through this year's project.

I am A

Peacer

KOSOVO'S HEALTH KIT CAMPAIGN

cert. done.   left msg. 2x4.

DATE: Apr. 16/99

INTERESTED: (YES)   NO

SCHOOL/ORGANIZATION NAME: Westmount Collegiate Institute

CONTACT NAME: Stephen Bloom, Mr. John Charlton

ADDRESSS: Atkinson & Bathurst (just N of Bathurst & Centre)
1000 New Westminster D. Suite 103
THORNHILL   L4J 8G3
*World Issues Class Mrs Lori Cristillo sez she'll send her class
to McDonald House one AM next week

PHONE # (905)882-0277 ~~ext.~~ School; ~~905~~ (416) 638-7700 Home

FAX # (905) 882-2450

TOTAL NUMBER OF KITS: 30 or so kits, lots of other materials, $260

OTHER ITEMS: STUFFED ANIMALS a few

BABY ITEMS a lot (10 bags of diapers, toys, etc)

CHILDREN'S ITEMS

TO BE PICKED UP: Monday, April 19, 1999 2pm-3pm

INVENTORY FORM FOR HEALTH & SCHOOL KITS

D: 16-11-01
ED: 14

school kits:
health kits:
plete kits:
i kits
books

Extra Supplies:

RECEIVED FROM:
NAME OF CONTACT PERSON: Miriam Datskovsky
NAME OF THE ORGANIZATION:
ADDRESS: The Shipley School
814 Yarrow St.
Bryn Mawr PA 19010
June 11, 2001

INVENTORY DATE:

Health kits
Face towel
Wash cloth
Toothbrush
Toothpaste
Comb
scissors
Band-aids
Bar of soap

United States Postal Service
Customs Declaration and Dispatch Note

Sender's Name and Address (Nom et adresse de l'expéditeur)
Miriam Datskovsky
The Shipley School
814 Yarrow St
Bryn Mawr PA 19010

Addressee's Name and Address (Nom et adresse du destinataire)
Free The Children
1750 Steeles Ave West, So
Concord Ontario
Canada L4K 2L7

List of Contents (Désignation du contenu) Please Print | Qty. | Value (Valeur) | Net Weight (Poids net)
School Supplies
16-1533544 (Charitable Status #) | | $10 | 22 lbs

Insured No. | Insured Amount US $ | SDR Insured Value | Postage US $ | Gross Weight
| | | | 22 oz

Commercial Sample (Echantillon commercial) ☐ Documents ☐ Gift (Cadeau) ☐ Merchandise

Sender's Signature and Date (Signature de l'expéditeur et date)
Miriam M. Datskovsky

the particulars given in the customs declaration are correct
not contain any dangerous article prohibited by

June 11, 99

This is to certify that the
Red Cross received 870 health
kits from Kids Can Free
The Children.
Paul Bookman

INVENTORY FORM FOR HEALTH & SCHOOL KITS

DATE RECEIVED: MAY 18
ITEMS RECEIVED:
Complete school kits: 2
Complete health kits: 2

Incomplete kits:
School kits:
Notebooks
Ruler
Scissors
Eraser
Pencils
Pencil Sharpener
Crayons or colour pencils
Coloured construction paper
Tennis ball
Cloth bag

Health kits
Face towel
Wash cloth
Toothbrush
Toothpaste
Comb
Nail file
Band-aid
Bar of soap

RECEIVED FROM:
NAME OF CONTACT PERSON: Jessie Rice
NAME OF THE ORGANIZATION:
ADDRESS: 115 Dogwood F-K
NIPPA KY 41240

INVENTORY DATE: May 18
DATE SENT BY FREE THE CHILDREN:
ADDRESS SENT TO:

Laila Primary School was the second major schoolbuilding project completed by Free The Children in a Maasai community. The school is home to children ranging in ages from as young as 3 years old all the way up to 19 years, providing education from nursery school up to Standard (Grade) 8. About 220 students in total, Laila is one of our smaller schools in the region.

Laila is an impressive building, equipped with beautiful and clean accommodations for teachers—a rarity in the region, as many schools built by the government provide nothing more than mud shacks for teachers. Since the official inauguration of Laila many years ago, teachers have been more readily attracted to teach within the Maasai community due to the improved facilities. Set up in a quadrant-style layout, the school lies at the base of one of the miniscule "mountain" ranges in the region, bordering another community.

All classrooms are clean and spacious, kept cool by stone walls, featuring big twisted metal framed pane windows, secured with a roof that even contains skylights! The desks are made out of wood and metal, painted white by a local woman who is in charge of fulfilling all the orders to ensure that each child has a comfortable place to sit and learn while in class. The blackboard is real (not just a piece of plywood painted black), stocked with colored chalk, erasers and laminated multiplication and square root tables, facts about the nearby mountain ranges, the ecosystem and different ways to recycle raw materials.

- Charlotte Sobolewski

"Ordinary People can do EXTRAordinary things with Support."

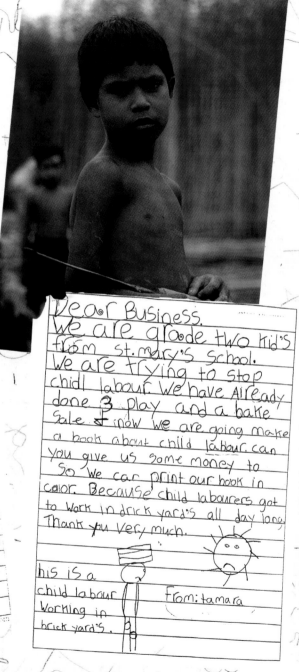

Dear Business
We are grade two students from
t St. mary's Sexsmith we are trying
to stop child labour we have had
a bake sale & some plays & the
play's that we have done are
the three little pig the little red
hen & the Ginger bread man for child
labour. we are going to make a
book about child labour to let
other peaple know about child labour
so that more peaple will help.
Some child labourers lift hevy
bricks. can you prease donate money
to print our book in color the child
labours work all day! we hope you
can help. Thank you.

from: Hailey 8 years old

Dear Business,
We are grade two kid's
from st. mary's school.
We are trying to stop
chidl labour. We have Already
done 3 play and a bake
Sale & now we are going make
a book about child labour. can
you give us some money to
So We car print our book in
color. Because child labourers got
to Work in drick yard's all day long.
Thank you very much.

his is a
child labour
Working in
brick yard's.

From: tamara

145

Toronto Star - Nov. 13, 2000

It's time 16-year-olds were given the right to vote

BY CRAIG KIELBURGER

Recently, a special *Studio Two* TVO broadcast examined the issue of globalization with representatives from government, business, unions and the media.

A young woman from the audience raised her hand to ask a question. "Where are you from?" asked host Steve Pagan.

"I'm from B.C.," she replied.

"Did you ever vote for Glen Clark?" he inquired.

"I'm not old enough to vote," she answered.

"And your question?"

"I was wondering if John Crosbie can comment on what his opinion is on the way in which the WTO has integrated developing nations into the platform of globalizing trade and if the panel could comment on the ramifications that it has had for these countries."

Like Jasmine, the young woman in the audience, tens of thousands of intelligent 16- and 17-year-old Canadians, who are deeply interested in issues such as poverty, homelessness, debt reduction, education and globalization, will be denied the right to have a voice through their vote in the upcoming municipal and federal elections.

Section 50 of the Canada Elections Act states that only Canadian citizens who have attained the age of 18 on or before the day of election are allowed to vote.

"Young people are not knowledgeable or mature enough to form their own opinions at 16," are comments one hears frequently.

I beg to differ. Today, young people are more exposed to information than any other generation. Issues like NAFTA, free trade, the International Monetary Fund, the World Trade Organization are being discussed in schools at a younger and younger age as students use the Internet to search the government and university libraries around the world.

There is no magic age when an individual becomes an ideal citizen. Indeed, there are ignorant or indifferent people of all ages. I submit that most individuals at age 16 do have the maturity and intelligence required to vote.

Many 16-year-olds have part-time jobs and pay taxes. All pay PST and GST. Should they not also have a say as to how their tax dollars are spent?

It is obvious that if young people had the vote, political parties would take them more seriously. Consider how little discussion there has been in this federal election (and the one in

1997) on child poverty, education, the environment and other youth-related issues. Topics arbitrarily decided upon by adults who are not directly affected by the decision-making process would find a new and more prominent place on political agendas. Who better to challenge the government on its record on children and youth issues than youth?

KIELBURGER

Canada was one of the first of 194 countries of the world to ratify the United Nations' Convention on the Rights of the Child that gives children (under the age of 18) the right to participate in finding solutions to issues affecting them and their peers. A 16- and 17-year-old group of voters would give a political voice to this entire segment of Canadian citizens for the first time in our democratic history. Empowering 16-year-olds with the vote would open the door to new respect for young people's opinions and an era of equality for all generations.

Current statistics indicate that approximately 75 per cent of first-time 18-year-old voters in Canada are not yet registered for the upcoming elec-

tions. Attaining the right to vote at 18 is too late. Many young people have already become apathetic about the political process. They feel powerless and believe that their thoughts and opinions do not really matter.

In North American society, companies compete for the disposable income of the young population, and spend millions of dollars in advertising and market studies to try to entice them to purchase their goods and services.

Ironically, however, politicians do not really take notice of young people until they are of voting age and thus important to their political success. Too frequently, token gestures are made to youth for the sake of appearances and the media.

Get them young! We should learn what cigarette companies already know: Habits formed in youth are difficult to break. Instilling in young people a sense of civic duty while still in high school would increase the overall voter turnout as the population ages.

Where do people learn about the democratic process and their civic responsibility as Canadians? Only 67 per cent of eligible adults voters cast their ballot in the last federal election and a mere one-third took the time to vote in municipal elections. How often do we hear adults say that they know

nothing about the political candidates in their area?

A lower voting age could be tied in with the current program in civics education in high school where political parties, issues and candidates are studied in depth. Active participation in the voting process with polling booths set up in schools during election periods would help to foster a lifetime of electoral participation.

Lowering the voting age to 16 is not a novel idea. Brazil has recently given the right to vote at all levels of government to 16-year-olds in that country. France, England and Australia are also contemplating lowering the voting age.

Last month, I attended meetings with world leaders at the State of the World Forum in New York City and talked to the Japanese minister of finance about youth issues during a trip to Japan. On Nov. 27, however, I shall be denied the right to cast my vote for the individual I believe should lead my own country. Why? Because I am 17 years old.

The time has come for Canadians to take a serious look at lowering the voting age to 16.

Craig Kielburger is founder and chairperson of (Kids Can) Free the Children.

Artwork by Jenn Gorotiza,
Grade 11

In Grade 6 I read [Craig's] book about Free The Children and [his] voyage to India! At that moment I realized that I don't have to wait to be an adult to get socially involved. I started to get in contact with Free The Children. Every e-mail took me a long time to write in English but I was so happy when I got an answer.

I realized that Free The Children has already grown and that there are groups all around the world. The fact that there were already so many groups of youth gave me courage to start a Free The Children chapter in Switzerland. Before I told my friends about it, I wanted to really inform myself what Free The Children was about and especially what child labour was. After approximately half a year, I told my friend Fiorina about it. Surprisingly she had the same idea and we started Free The Children-Switzerland. Without knowing what we were actually doing we got more and more members and organized small projects like an Indian dinner, a benefit concert, and flea markets…

It has now been more than four years since we started Free The Children-Switzerland. A few weeks ago we even donated $3,000 to a schoolbuilding project in Sierra Leone.

- Saskia Beck

THE WHITE HOUSE

WASHINGTON

March 7, 1996

Craig Kielburger
Free the Children
16 Thornbank Road
Thornhill
Ontario L4J2A2
CANADA

Dear Craig:

I recently saw an article about you in The Washington Post. I know that many Americans share your outrage at the tragic story of Iqbal Masih, and I'm very impressed by your campaign against child labor abuses.

Young people are our most profound responsibility, and I am committed to protecting their health and well-being -- both within the United States and throughout the world. It is a travesty that children in many countries are forced into full-time labor and often are subjected to harsh working conditions and other abuses. By supporting initiatives such as RUGMARK and the Child Labor Deterrence Act, by encouraging strict trade agreements, and by promoting the development of safe working conditions, my Administration is working hard to implement international child labor protections.

The United States is also using its membership in the International Labor Organization and in the World Trade Organization -- the body administering the GATT -- to encourage member states to discuss workers' rights and the issue of child labor. In addition, for the past two years, the U.S. Department of Labor has been investigating the plight of child workers around the world, particularly those involved in the production of goods imported into the United States. The Department has published its results in a comprehensive report, By the Sweat and Toil of Children, which will continue to raise public awareness of international child labor abuses.

The courageous work of young people like you is vitally important, and I am grateful for your efforts to honor Iqbal's memory. Best wishes for much continued success.

Sincerely,

Bill Clinton

Have Fun!

Stay motivated. At times, you may even run into some opposition. When this happens, try to remember why you got involved in the first place. Your goal is to help others make a difference.

Once you have finished your campaign or event, throw a pizza party or go to a movie with your team. Also, do not be afraid of having fun while you are organizing your activities. Try not to lose focus of the task at hand, but do not forget to make your social involvement an enjoyable and memorable experience.

SEE! I told you I could fly!

What do you think Jilleen? Should I throw him over?

Sometimes people say to me,

"It must be thrilling to meet famous people."

It is true, I have met many well-known people in my recent travels with Free The Children—Pope John Paul II, Shimon Perez, Jane Goodall, Queen Elizabeth II, former U.S. vice president Al Gore, the Dalai Lama and others. It was exciting, I have to admit. But it is not the memories of meeting these people that I cherish most. Nor are they the ones who have been my greatest inspiration...

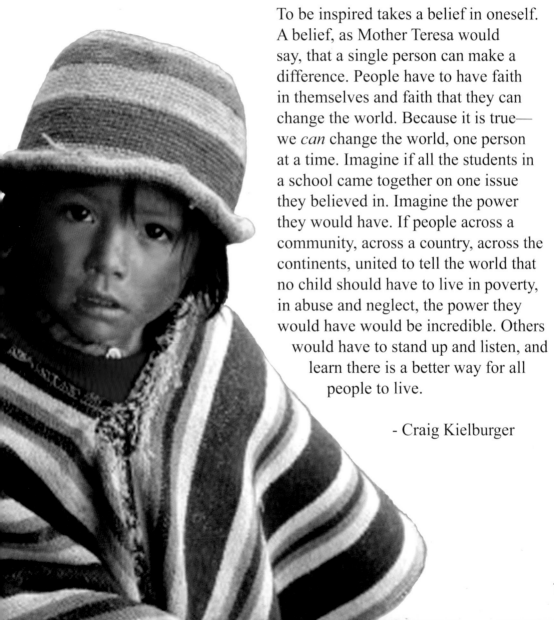

...It is the children I've met who are my real heroes. It is their courage and hope for a better world that rings clearest in my mind. When I am discouraged, it is the memories of these young people that I return to for faith in what I am doing.

To be inspired takes a belief in oneself. A belief, as Mother Teresa would say, that a single person can make a difference. People have to have faith in themselves and faith that they can change the world. Because it is true— we *can* change the world, one person at a time. Imagine if all the students in a school came together on one issue they believed in. Imagine the power they would have. If people across a community, across a country, across the continents, united to tell the world that no child should have to live in poverty, in abuse and neglect, the power they would have would be incredible. Others would have to stand up and listen, and learn there is a better way for all people to live.

- Craig Kielburger

For the last four whirlwind years, Free The Children has given me the tools I need to become the change I want to experience in the world. Being incapable of highlighting all the opportunities I have had because of this organization, I'll focus on just one in particular.

Understand how easy it is for us to get caught up in academia, refusing to see outside the essays, the GPA, the scholarship applications, the final exams. Free The Children has been an incredible outlet for me and many of my fellow students to utilize our education, be it international relations, music or biology, and actually SEE the results of our efforts.

- Erin Blanding

The true inspiration came when I started to meet all the members of Free The Children. These youth, many of whom were my age, were so passionate and so committed to their beliefs. They weren't forced into it, and there was no motive behind their actions except that they truly wanted to help people and make a difference. It was then that I realized that being socially involved was something that anyone can do, as long as you have passion.

- Jason Apostol

156

Artwork by Christina, Kendall, and Brittany

Julia, Rebecca and Aimée.

Dear Free the Children

Here is all the money that we raised from the second-hand sale that we did, on the 28th of May 2002 at our school. We managed to raise £300. We hope this will be lots of help!

Sorry this has taken so long to get to you, but we had to develope the film so we could send you the lovely picture of us and the sale! We would be grateful if you would reply to us when you recive this letter and money. By either E-mail or post: ~~█████~~ @ yahoo.co.uk. or Julia, Becky and Aimée.

~~████████~~

All the best,

Julia, Aimée
xx   xxx
x

Rebecca
xx
x

the future

The Future

It has been many years now since the United Nations Convention on the Rights of the Child became the most widely ratified human-rights treaty in history. Today, the world is still struggling to live up to the convention's promises. Well over 100 million children have never been to school, and many are being denied the resources they need to survive:

- 1 in 2 children still live in poverty
- 1 in 3 live without adequate shelter
- 1 in 5 does not have access to safe drinking water
- 1 in 6 is involved in child labor
- 1 in 7 does not have access to medical care

If the struggle for children's rights is now more urgent than ever, young people's determination to create a more just and compassionate world grows stronger as well. The challenges before us today may be enormous, but so are our reserves of passion, creativity and energy.

In looking toward the future, we must never forget that the greatest victories have always been won by those with the courage to dream, the passion to believe and the intensity to act. The many who struggled for civil rights, fought against apartheid, and worked to end the cruelties of colonialism were initially scorned as idealists. Though they faced opposition, they never stopped working toward the future they believed in, they never ceased to trust that their efforts mattered.

We have proven that change is possible, and we must prove this anew each time we act. In charting our course, we must never lose sight of the kind of world in which we want to live. We must ensure that our legacy is a reflection not of the obstacles we face, but the ideals we cherish.

Artwork by Natalie Camacho
and Jennifer Hansen

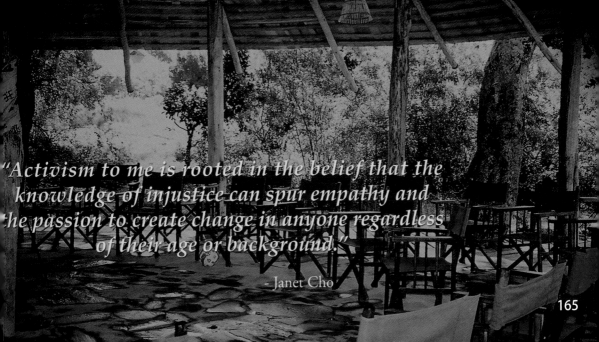

"Although my approach to activism has evolved since my first taste of it when I was 13, the fundamental way in which I view activism is rooted in my experiences with Free The Children, shaped largely by the inspiring young people I have met and the mentors that I have had the privilege of learning from."

"My conception of activism is one that is not exclusive to the Che Guevera incarnates, militant anarchists, and Bob Geldofs, people often associate with activism today. Instead, it is broadened by my realization that young people can be powerful agents of change, often contributing their own unique perspectives, creativity, and youthful vitality to their efforts whether it is through small but important actions such as informing others about the value of recycling or advocating for policy change in one's government."

"Activism to me is rooted in the belief that the knowledge of injustice can spur empathy and the passion to create change in anyone regardless of their age or background."

- Janet Cho

Five weeks have passed since I made a transition I never thought that I would make. I never saw myself sharing a room with a complete stranger, living in downtown Toronto. I never envisioned working for less than a secretary after completing both an undergraduate and a post-graduate degree. I never dreamed that I would give up my car in favour of public transportation. Turns out that "life is what happens when you are making other plans."

It took the discovery of a book, and the chance to help an organization using the skills I had gained through my many years of education, to show me a path I never dreamed of. And so it is. The idea that your future can be determined in a moment is one that is certainly not believed by many. I will not deny that my experiences growing up serving, coaching, reading and questioning did not affect my future path, but I do feel that when I felt for the first time that I had a general sense of where I was going, my course changed in the blink of an eye, or rather the turning of several hundred pages.

There are no limits to this path. It can provide countless opportunities, tremendous contacts and the chance to serve on a greater level. I can now think of nothing more exciting than loving what I do and reaching out across the globe to help others reach the same realization and their same potential.

- Caileigh Dauphinais

Artwork by Courtney Sanela

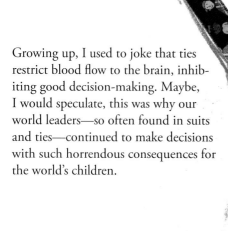

Growing up, I used to joke that ties restrict blood flow to the brain, inhibiting good decision-making. Maybe, I would speculate, this was why our world leaders—so often found in suits and ties—continued to make decisions with such horrendous consequences for the world's children.

Over the years, this tie has traveled around the world. It has often appeared before U.S. Congressional Sub-Committees, Canadian Parliamentary Hearings and United Nations conferences. It has been present at the State of the World Forum and the World Economic Forum, and attended countless banquets, dinners and functions.

Eventually, I grudgingly began to don a tie myself—but only when absolutely necessary. As a gesture of protest, I always wore the same one. It was blue, and covered with drawings of children from different ethnic backgrounds. I hoped my colorful statement would remind our leaders to consider the impact of their actions on children across the globe.

- Craig Kielburger

Free The Children provides young people with a sense of purpose, a sense of motivation to action and a sense of humility when faced with the lives of so many people around the world. Free The Children challenges young people to see the world more clearly and more closely.

Working against child labor is a lot more important when you know the names and stories of specific children. Working against child prostitution is more heart breaking and infinitely more imperative when you've met Jessica and know what happened to her. Free The Children has always had the ability to make largely social struggles much more personal: to bring "global issues" into people's lives in a way that says, "you can't forget about me, this is important."

Currently, I'm living in Morogoro, Tanzania, serving as a United States Peace Corps volunteer. Peace Corps volunteers serve two-year contracts, and the first year is as notoriously difficult as the second year is famously rewarding. The first year is about figuring things out, learning the language, the culture, the community and all the little basic things that make up life anywhere.

The second year, things start falling into place, and you start being able to really feel that you're getting work done. The language is more accessible, the culture more familiar and the community becomes home. At least that's what I've been told, and I sure hope that's how it works. Right now, I'm smack in the middle of the first year, and quite frankly, it's kicking my butt.

Moving to Africa, it turns out, is not easy. Apparently I ignored that memo. But I draw a lot of my motivation to keep one foot in front of the other from the time I spent with Free The Children, and the commitment and drive I remember from my friends there. What a fantastic, nurturing and inspiring community our beloved tribe provides, even so many years out.

This is not easy work that we ask of ourselves. As easy as it is to be overwhelmed by the scale of need and daily difficulty of getting work done in developing countries, the opposite is also treacherous. It is so easy to become disconnected from the work that we do: to become disconnected from the reasons why we do it, or from the people for whom we do it.

It can be much easier to be satisfied with the feeling that we have done work than with the results of the work itself. The devil's temptation of activists is to make it so easy for our identities to be affirmed as people who "do good" before we have actually accepted the much more grueling but ultimately vital and infinitely more rewarding work of actually making the world a better place. How do you even reach for such a goal?

You let it in. You let the world in, and you let it get to you. But at the end of the day, we have a responsibility neither to be paralyzed by it, nor to be satisfied with our own personal growth. The good fight needs fighting too badly. The world needs us too badly. We have a responsibility to come back out swinging. And besides, it's a lot more fun that way.

- Dianna Hunter English

172

The Truth

I used to lie. Not a little—a lot. About what I thought, what I believed, what had happened to me the night before, and all for no reason that I could recognize at the time. But it was there, and I couldn't stop. It became this terrible trap, and I would spend my time stressed out over who I told what to and worrying if they would talk to each other. I'm not ashamed about it, and I know a lot of young people go through it. Only now do I realize why I chose to lie instead of tell the truth.

When talking about Me to We and Free The Children, as well as the larger scale of social involvement, I often choose to tell stories from my first trip with Me to We. It is the story I tell in most of my speeches of how I got involved and when I started to see a bigger picture. But it was over four years ago that I got involved with this place. I say "this place" for a reason—I am sitting right in it. At this very moment, I am sitting at my desk at 233 Carlton St., Toronto, Ontario, first level, sitting with my feet up on my chair, drinking a cup of fair trade coffee from the java place across the street. It's 3:37 p.m. Why am I here NOW? That is a question I have less practice answering.

I'm here because it's unpredictable: one day I'm at a school working with a group of amazing teenagers on volunteering and social issues, the next I am at a concert put on by youth to raise money and awareness for war-affected children. I am here because the feeling I get from working for something pure and good is one I haven't found anywhere else. I am here because the people I work with are unlike any others I have met in my life.

There are a lot more of us than there used to be, but every individual is so special. We all come from varied backgrounds, with different experiences and values, and even different senses of humor. But somehow, or maybe because of this, we are one family. We've heard the story of the Minga, and never have I seen such a demonstration as I do here, with every project we take on. We make decisions together, we discuss ideas together, we execute plans together, we bust our butts together, we celebrate our accomplishments together. Whatever comes our way, we are in it. Together. I'm here because never have I had a group of people believe in me as much, trust me as much and make me feel as loved and accepted as I do here.

I used to lie because I didn't feel good enough. I don't lie anymore, and I haven't in a long time. There is no need. Because of the people I have met through Free The Children and Me to We and the confidence I have gained through their love and friendship, I have no reason to mask what I believe or who I am. They love everyone for who they are. True story.

- Julia Crabbe

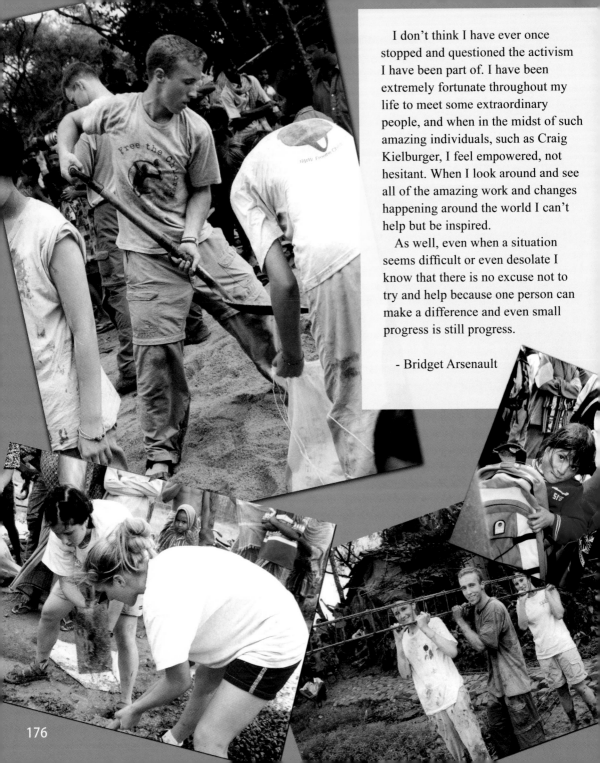

I don't think I have ever once stopped and questioned the activism I have been part of. I have been extremely fortunate throughout my life to meet some extraordinary people, and when in the midst of such amazing individuals, such as Craig Kielburger, I feel empowered, not hesitant. When I look around and see all of the amazing work and changes happening around the world I can't help but be inspired.

As well, even when a situation seems difficult or even desolate I know that there is no excuse not to try and help because one person can make a difference and even small progress is still progress.

- Bridget Arsenault

The most rewarding experiences always involve young people. I love working with young people and seeing all of the amazing work that they do. It's always so inspiring when I'm working with Free The Children and I see other Youth in Action groups taking a stance on something that they believe in.

- Bridget Arsenault

Artwork by Michael Casimir,
Bobby Abbate, Ethan Breenberg,
Martin G Figueroa, Jr, 7th Grade

177

The last 10 years have meant **accomplishments**. Yes, super huge ones like Nobel Peace Prize nominations and **partnerships** with Oprah and meetings with Mother Teresa, the Pope, the Queen of England and the Prime Minister, but the accomplishments—the true accomplishments—can be found in the smiles of the kids who now have the **confidence to smile**.

- Kim Plewes

Artwork by Raisha Gates

FREE THE CHILDREN
EXCEPTO LOS NIÑOS
AUBER DEN KINDERN
RISPARMI I BAMBINI
EXCEPTO AS CRIANÇA
SAUVEZ LES ENFANTS

Let's Move From Me To We

Twinkle, twinkle little star—what do I do?

The world's a disaster, the worst has come true.

Hungry children, homeless children, children fighting wars

While the greedy tell the needy: "We know that you're poor,

But that's just the way it is now, nothing's going to change

If you try to fight, people will think you're strange."

So why should I believe that I can change the world?

If you look at me now you see I'm just one girl.

So first I and me need to become a fighting We

Need to become a loving team of generosity

By each of us waking up tomorrow with a smile

And knowing we're alive but only for a while

The power of choice is the power of voice.

by Louise Kent

My generation has a legacy to leave. We can choose for that legacy to be a continuation of poverty, of apathy, of neglect, or we can be remembered as the generation that brought an end to poverty, that brought smiles to the faces of the millions of children in our world, that did not allow people to die because there was not enough food.

We are making progress, but only if we keep working.

- Danielle Hoegy

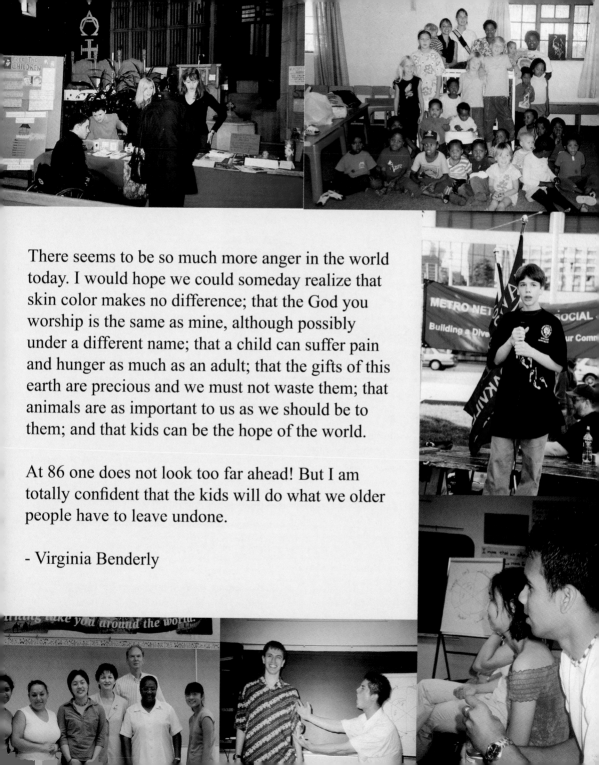

There seems to be so much more anger in the world today. I would hope we could someday realize that skin color makes no difference; that the God you worship is the same as mine, although possibly under a different name; that a child can suffer pain and hunger as much as an adult; that the gifts of this earth are precious and we must not waste them; that animals are as important to us as we should be to them; and that kids can be the hope of the world.

At 86 one does not look too far ahead! But I am totally confident that the kids will do what we older people have to leave undone.

- Virginia Benderly

A Final Word

In showcasing the talents, dreams and accomplishments of those who have helped Free The Children become all that it has over the years, this book reminds us of an important truth: we all have a unique contribution to make when it comes to building a better world. Thank you Lekha for spreading the word through the voices of young people themselves!

This book represents far more than a celebration of past accomplishments—it is a call to action. I hope that the words and images that spring from its pages will inspire others to discover their own spark, and put their passion and talents to good use.

–Craig and Marc Kielburger

Ten Ways to Make a Difference

1. Visit our websites at www.freethechildren.com and www.metowe.com to learn more.

2. **Adopt a Village:** Join Free The Children's Adopt a Village campaign and support community development in marginalized rural communities around the world.

3. **Build a School:** Get involved in Free The Children's Brick by Brick: Schoolbuilding project to build new schools, repair damaged ones, furnish classrooms and provide for teachers.

4. **Start a Youth in Action Group:** Become a Youth in Action Group member and join in fundraising, learning about issues and raising awareness about children's rights.

5. **Donate:** Support Free The Children's efforts with a monetary or in-kind donation and know that your generosity will make a difference to those in need in communities around the world.

6. **Volunteer Overseas:** Volunteer overseas with Me to We Trips and gain practical, on-the-ground experience in developing countries.

7. **Invite a Speaker:** Arrange for Craig or Marc Kielburger or another Me to We Speaker to inspire your school, church, business or community organization.

8. **Live the Me to We Philosophy:** Reach out to others by focusing less on "me" and more on "we"—our communities, our nation and our world. Visit www.metowe.com to learn more.

9. **Attend the Take Action Academy:** Participate in our annual week-long Take Action! Academy and learn how to work toward positive social change while having a blast!

10. **Participate in the Halloween for Hunger campaign:** Join family and friends in fighting hunger by trick-or-treating for non-perishable goods instead of candy next Halloween.

To learn about other exciting ways to get involved, visit our websites at www.freethechildren.com and www.metowe.com.

Before

After

Free The Children Has...

- Built more than 500 schools in 16 countries providing education for 50,000 children every day
- Shipped more than $15 million worth of medical supplies and provided health care to more than 512,500 people
- Equipped more than 23,500 women with alternative income initiatives
- Provided clean water to more than 138,500 people in various developing countries.

Four billion human beings... young + old, sick + well, happy + un- happy, kind and unkind, strong + weak, people every- where are all different. It's very strange; some people even hate others because they are different. They forget that they too would

by: Jessica Chollis Allie Lasswell Text by: Peter Spier

Seem different if they could only see themselves through other peoples eyes But imagine how dull this world would be if everybody would look, think, dress, and act the same Isn't it wonderful that everybody is different from each other.

188

Artwork by Jessica Chollis, Allie Lasswell, and Peter Spier

My biggest worry when I became involved in issues of social justice was that I would be alone, working against a force too big to make a significant dent in. In the past four years, through my work with Free The Children, I have been convinced that the huge force at work is a movement of non-apathetic youth...youth seeing positive action change from an idealistic dream into an incredible reality. Being a part of this movement is all the inspiration I require to keep pushing forward.

- Erin Blanding

The future is a call to action.

Alternative Income Project

In one village in India, Free The Children has provided 500 women with milking animals and 153 women with sewing machines and gem polishing machines, which have significantly improved their standards of living. Ms. Jayaraman and her husband used to work as marginalized agriculture day laborers in Thiruvanrangapatty village in Tamil Nadu, India. They earned a combined income of a meager 800 rupees, or $15 US per month, during seasonal times. The Jayaraman family lived below the poverty line, and their struggle worsened during the off-season or during periodic droughts, when it was even more difficult to find work. It was the children who suffered the most. They were often hungry and were unable to attend school since their parents could not afford the supplies and uniforms necessary to attend the government school. In efforts to improve the standards of living of the families in Thiruvanrangapatty village, and to enable children in this village to realize their right to basic education, Free The Children provided poor families with a sustainable source of income by supplying them with milking animals and small machines. The Jayaraman family was

one such family, and they were provided with a milking cow worth $250 US in 2000. Almost three and a half years later, the Jayaraman family, which once struggled for existence below the poverty line, was enjoying a standard of living that was well above that of most of their fellow villagers. Their children are now attending school, while the family's income has more than tripled because of their participation in Free The Children's Alternative Income projects. With expenses estimated at approximately $45 US per month, the family, for the first time, has a disposable source of income, something which was unimaginable just a few years ago.

At Free The Children the message was loud and clear: "You have the power to be a catalyst for social change, and we challenge you to be a powerful catalyst."

- Vanessa Nicholas

The people that I have met and the experiences that I have had through my travels have also allowed me to realize that we should not consider ourselves to be saviours or superior beings to those living in poverty and suffering from hunger, because once we engage in actions that help others, it is not a one-way street. It is not only we who impart all the wisdom, it is not only us who have the capacity to help, but it is also those whom we are helping who have the potential to help themselves, who have that ability to realize their capacity to become empowered, and who can teach us a few things about being human—about happiness, about love, about sharing.

- Janet Cho

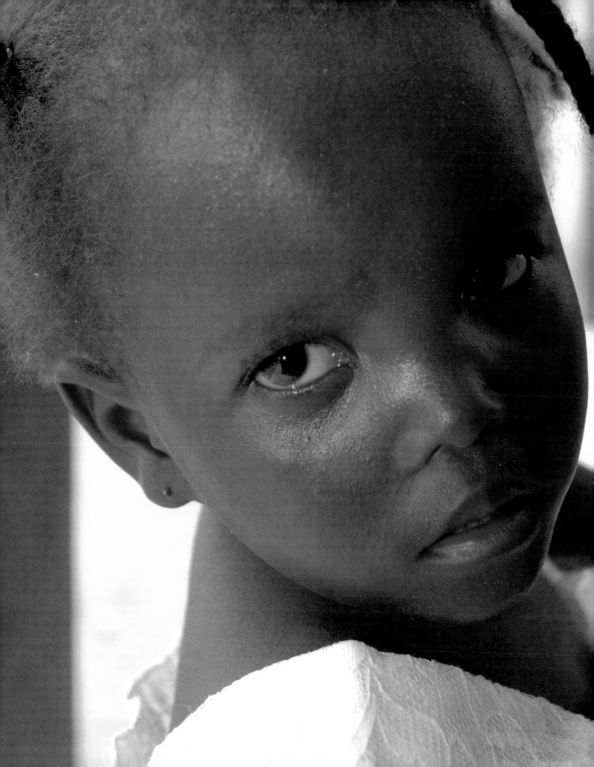

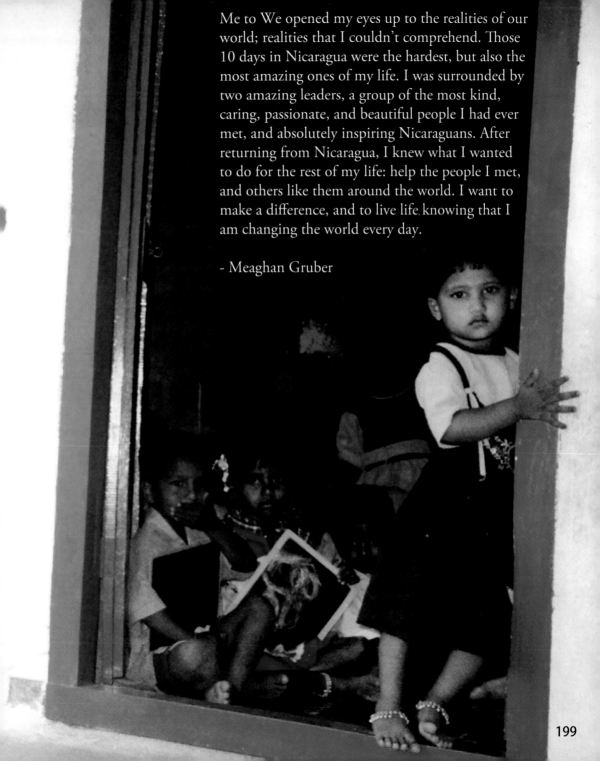

Me to We opened my eyes up to the realities of our world; realities that I couldn't comprehend. Those 10 days in Nicaragua were the hardest, but also the most amazing ones of my life. I was surrounded by two amazing leaders, a group of the most kind, caring, passionate, and beautiful people I had ever met, and absolutely inspiring Nicaraguans. After returning from Nicaragua, I knew what I wanted to do for the rest of my life: help the people I met, and others like them around the world. I want to make a difference, and to live life knowing that I am changing the world every day.

- Meaghan Gruber

FRISCO

My interest in the environment started when I was about 9, when my step-father told me to turn off the lights. I asked him why, and he said that it is a waste of energy. He explained to me in depth that if global warming got any worse that the ice caps would melt, the weather would bring more and more tornados (which I was terrified of), we might have to move (living close to the coast). He told me to watch the weather seasonally, if I could tell the difference each year. I did, with ease. That's when I became an activist and decided to take small steps that would decrease the impact I have on the environment. I started to do all of the little things: taking staggered showers, turning water off when I brushed my teeth, riding my bike, and car-pooling.

It wasn't until recently that I started to move beyond staggered showers, dark rooms, and "sleeping" computers and onto actions I could take to get other people to join me. How could I get as many people as I could to help out the environment and take little steps? I started to talk to people about what we should do to help Mother Nature heal herself back up. I told them to start and try to do all of these things and explained the impact they would have. I gave them statistics and tangible examples that they could relate to.

I joined a group called Students Taking Action. Every Thursday, we meet and talk about what we want for our school. One main focus is raising awareness for the environment.

Right now our school only recycles about half of the paper we use, and nothing else. I want the administration to know what the benefits of recycling in our school are. We can get money from a nearby recycling center that will pay us for every ton of paper we recycle. If we do this, there are a few organizations that will give us grants to strengthen our recycling program. The people of Peterborough would pay attention, and we might be able to spread what we have done throughout the town.

We're also teaching our peers about the health and environmental benefits of becoming a vegetarian: saving massive amounts of water and food that could help other people, saving land space, a healthier heart rate, and a sense of empathy towards mass-produced animals.

My step-father explained to me as a child that people are responsible for the environment, and I related this to my passion and deep interest in Africa. He told me that the continent would shrink, a lot of the people and culture would die down, the natural resources would be lessened, possibly stirring violence in countries that rely on the resources. He told me that the land that didn't get covered in water probably would become desert and uninhabitable if we kept using energy without empathetic thought of who we are affecting.

But the climate change that is reality for Africa is also reality for where you are right now. You and I are responsible for our actions, and we can also help create a bigger change through inspiring others. It's like Mahatma Gandhi says: "You must be the change you wish to see in the world."

-- Frisco Pucciarello

I **always got involved** with a lot of things. But it was Free The Children, in high school, that really hit me hard. It took my activism to new heights.

Soon after I joined, I began giving speeches for FTC. I spoke about child labor and prostitution work and children. The kids would put up their hands and say, "Have you ever met these kids?" And one day, some smart-aleck kid put up his hand and said, "What gives you the authority to talk on behalf of these kids?"

That's when I realized: maybe it's time that I go and do this myself. I had read enough. I just needed to go and learn more. After a while, you read and you read and you do as much research as you can. But you want to meet the kids behind the stats.

My parents trusted me enough to let me go. I arranged with my school to spend three months in Sri Lanka, where I would work with organizations there to see what life is like for exploited children. I was 17, and what I saw would forever change my life.

My main objective was to see with my own eyes, talk to the kids, hear their stories, and ask them what young people can do to help.

Even just walking through the slums, I would have to opportunity to go into some of the houses, which were shacks essentially, and just talk to families. "What can we do? I'm a young person from Canada. I'm Sri Lankan, just like you. But what can I do, what can other people do, to help?"

I found that, whether it's Sri Lanka, whether it's the Philippines, it doesn't matter—the answers are always the same: they say, "Tell everybody what happened to us. Spread the word so that kids in the next generation don't have to go through this."

Some friends and I decided the way to tell everybody was to get Air Canada to show an in-flight video about the issue of child exploitation. This was the first project of OneChild. It took a lot of hard work to get such a big company to see us and to take us seriously as an organization of young people. And when we finally got the appointment, the first thing they wanted was a sample video.

We had one week, so we borrowed a camera, wrangled all our friends, and made the video with zero budget. We were still in editing as we drove to Air Canada's headquarters.

A week later we got the call: it was a yes. Our video is now seen by 400,000 passengers every month and has inspired young people around the world to join our movement.

Before I joined Free The Children, all I knew was that I was doing something good. Now I realize that what I was doing was activism. ■

Cheryl Perera

Afterword

After many years of learning and growing together, this is a wonderful time to reflect on how far we've come, celebrate our achievements and look toward the future. It seems like only yesterday that a group of 12-year-olds set out to change the world—more than a decade later Free The Children is the world's largest network of children helping children through education. As we have grown, we have remained committed to working to free children everywhere from poverty, exploitation and powerlessness. We have learned so much so quickly—both about the world and ourselves—and have had the time of our lives in the process! The years have been filled with excitement, countless moments of joy, lots of hard work and more than a few surprises.

This book draws upon the voices and talents of many members of the Free The Children family. It is a testament to the passion and courage of the world's young people and their dedication to building a better world. Thank you Lekha for documenting our journey—your talent and generosity have truly brought our story to life! The letters, artwork and personal stories collected here have come from all over the world. Each page has been lovingly crafted, and reflects a multitude of opinions, hopes and dreams. We can think of no better way to celebrate Free The Children's accomplishments and the ideals that inspire them.

We would like to extend a heartfelt thank you to everyone who has joined the Free The Children family over the years. Congratulations to all who have made this book possible!

Craig Kielburger
Founder and Chair
Free The Children

Marc Kielburger
Co-Founder
Free The Children

Our Work: Adopt a Village

Free The Children's holistic Adopt a Village approach to development means changes are long-lasting and sustainable. Through your help and donations, we work at home and overseas in the following areas:

 Building schools
We've built 500 schools to date, providing daily education to more than 50,000 young people. Our goal is to keep building schools until primary education is accessible to all children.

 Supporting health care
By providing basic medical needs and educating people on preventive health measures, we build healthier, stronger families and societies.

Providing alternative income resources

We provide disadvantaged women and their families with means of making an income, allowing their children to attend school instead of working.

Ensuring clean water and sanitation

Our clean water wells are built close to schools, so girls can study and fetch water at the same time. These wells stop the spread of disease that comes from contaminated water sources.

Empowering young leaders to be the change

Through domestic empowerment programs and leadership training, Free The Children inspires young people to develop as socially conscious global citizens and become agents of change for their peers around the world.

Even a little help makes an impact, and goes a long way in brightening the futures of disadvantaged families.

me to we
SPEAKERS

Bring a speaker to your child's school, your parent and educator association or your workplace conferences—and take away all you need to 'be the change.'

The team at Me to We Speakers has travelled the world to discover the most inspirational people with remarkable stories and life experiences.

From community activists to former child soldiers to social entrepreneurs, our roster of energetic, experienced speakers are leading the Me to We movement: living and working in developing communities, helping businesses achieve social responsibility and inspiring auditoriums of youth and educators to action. Their stories and powerful messages inspire, motivate and educate.

They leave audiences with a desire to take action and make a difference. They'll make you laugh, cry and gain new perspective on what really matters. Be warned: their passion is contagious!

Visit www.metowe.com/speakers to learn more.

ᴎᴎ me to we
TRIPS

If you want to really experience another culture and truly see the world, take a Me to We Trip.

Sure, you could lounge on yet another beach, surrounded by other stressed-out visitors seeing the usual tourist traps. But why not seek out a volunteer travel experience that radically changes your perspective, while positively transforming the lives of others? Our staff live and work in the communities you'll visit, coordinating schoolbuilding and supporting development in participation with local communities. On a Me to We Trip, you'll learn leadership skills, experience new cultures and forge truly meaningful connections.

Over 3,000 adventurous people of all ages have chosen to volunteer abroad with us. You'll do incredible things, like building schools and assisting on clean water projects. You'll meet exuberant children excited at new possibilities for learning, and be immersed in local communities in ways never otherwise possible.

You'll get your hands dirty, digging wells and laying foundations. But you'll love it. You'll come home with a sunburn—and the biggest smile you've ever had on your face. And best of all, you'll have memories that last a lifetime.

Visit www.metowe.com/trips to learn more.

211

The World Needs Your Kid: How to Raise Children Who Care and Contribute
Craig Kielburger and Marc Kielburger and Shelley Page

This unique guide to parenting is centred on a simple but profound philosophy that will encourage children to become global citizens. Drawing on life lessons from such remarkable individuals as Jane Goodall, Michael Douglas and Archbishop Desmond Tutu, award-winning journalist Shelley Page and Marc and Craig Kielburger demonstrate how small actions make huge differences in the life of a child and can ultimately change the world.

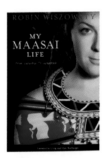

My Maasai Life
Robin Wiszowaty

In her early twenties Robin Wiszowaty left the ordinary world behind to join a traditional Maasai family. In the sweeping vistas and dusty footpaths of rural Kenya, she embraced a way of life unlike she'd ever known. With full-colour photographs from her adventures, Robin's heart-wrenching story will inspire you to question your own definitions of home, happiness and family.

Take Action! A Guide to Active Citizenship
Craig Kielburger and Marc Kielburger

Want to begin changing the world? *Take Action!* is a vivid, hands-on guide to active citizenship packed with the tools young people need to make a difference. Accomplished human rights activists Marc and Craig Kielburger share valuable tips and advice from their experiences as founders of Free The Children and the Me to We movement. Ideal for Grades 8–10, *Take Action!* shows that young people don't need to wait to be the leaders of tomorrow—this journey begins now.

Take More Action: How to Change the World
Craig Kielburger and Marc Kielburger with Deepa Shankaran

Ready to take the next step? *Take More Action* is our advanced guide to global citizenship, empowering young people to be world-changers—around the world or in their own backyard.

Brilliantly illustrated and packed with powerful quotes, stories and resources, *Take More Action* includes invaluable material on character education, ethical leadership, effective activism and global citizenship. Ideal for Grades 10 and up, *Take More Action* paves the way for a lifetime of social action.

Free the Children
Craig Kielburger

Written by Craig Kielburger on his return from Asia, *Free the Children* is the story that launched a movement. It tells the remarkable story of his encounters with some of the most disadvantaged children on earth, trapped in poverty and exploitative child labour. Winner of the prestigious Christopher Award, *Free the Children* has been translated into eight languages.

It Takes a Child
Craig Kielburger and Marisa Antonello; Illustrated by Turnstyle Imaging

It was an ordinary morning like any other. Twelve-year-old Craig Kielburger woke to his alarm clock and hurried downstairs to wolf down a bowl of cereal over the newspaper's comics before school. But what he discovered on the paper's front page would change his life—and eventually affect over a million young people worldwide.

It Takes a Child is a fun, vibrant look back at Craig's adventures throughout South Asia, learning about global poverty and child labour. This incredible story truly demonstrates you're never too young to change the world.

Visit www.metowe.com/books to learn more.

ACKNOWLEDGEMENTS

In true Free The Children spirit, this book represents the collective efforts of an extraordinary team of individuals we are honoured to call friends. Our deepest gratitude to Lekha Singh for all of her time, vision and leadership. This project would not have been possible without her.

A special thank you to Eva and Yoel Haller for their love, Michelle Douglas for her conviction; Dr. Dorothea Gaither for her insight and Dr. John Gaither for his thousands of hours spent volunteering. My appreciation to Rene Malo and his family, along with Clark Peterson and Jonathan Vanger for their dedication to sharing our story.

This book represents the experiences of Free The Children's more than fourteen years of work in the field of human rights and youth empowerment. We are especially grateful for the support of our board of directors, including Chris Besse, Mary Eileen Donovan, Charlotte Empey, Ed Gillis, Gregory Harmandayan, Adrian Horwood, Stephanie Kay, Kathy Sarafian, David Sersta, Lara Steinhouse, Jordana Weiss, Andrew Black, Juliet Bryan-Brown, David Cohen, Josh Cohen, Amy Eldon Turteltaub, Craig Heimark, Libby Heimark, Mary Lewis, Jessica Mayberry, Beverly Cooper Neufeld, Richard Prins, Ernan Roman, Hal Schwartz, Megan Sidhu, Dick Simon, Neil Taylor, Prof. Jonathan White, Monica Yunus, Heidi Hopper and Jim Baller.

And a special tribute to Virginia Benderly and Joe Opatowski, our friends whom we all miss dearly.

Our gratitude goes out to all the organizations and individuals who believe in Free The Children's mission. We would like to extend special thanks to Oprah Winfrey and Katy Davis from Harpo along with Caren Yanis, Tim Bennett, Annie Streer, Christina Timmins and Susan Thome from the Angel Network. We are thankful for the encouragement and support of Leonard Kurz and the Kurz Family Foundation; Julie Toskan-Casale and Diane Elliot from the Toskan Casale Foundation; Linda Rosier, Joe Catalano and the Colours of Freedom team; the Howie Stillman Young Leadership Fund; ONE X ONE; the Solo Family Foundation; the Boyd Foundation; the Journey Foundation; the Sanam Vaziri Quraishi Foundation; the Walter & Duncan Gordon Foundation; the Shapanski Family Foundation; The National Speakers Bureau; Michelle Lemmons and The International Speakers Bureau; the J.W. McConnell Family Foundation; Gerry Connelly, Chris Spence, Allan Hux, Mark Lowry and the Toronto District School Board students, principals and teachers; Taylor Gunn; Charlie Coffee; Bob French; Clive Metz; the Apostolopoulos family; the Joyal family; the Weiss Family; the Heimark family; the Rubin family; and Bob Lato and the Toronto Catholic District School Board.

We are privileged to count as friends Susan Antonacci and our friends at *Canadian Living*; Martin Regg Cohn and everyone at the *Toronto Star*; Odette and Cristelle Basmaji; Salim Khoja from Power-Within; Kim Mathewes from Klear Communications; Pi Media Partners; the i2 Foundation;

the Skoll Foundation; the Singh Foundation; Buzz Hargrove and the Canadian Auto Workers Union; David Krieger and the Nuclear Age Peace Foundation; dozens of remarkable educators including Greg Rogers, Mary-Eileen Donovan, Mark Fenwick, Nancy DiGregorio and Chris Spence; Karla Wilson and the School Voyageurs team; Larry Moore and the Ontario Library Association team; Lorraine Frost, Ron Common, Dennis Mock and the educators at Nipissing University; Veronica Atkins, Abby Bloch, Jacqueline Eberstein and the Robert C. and Veronica Atkins Foundation; and the entire team at CHUM Limited.

Much appreciation to our corporate and organizational partners, especially the team at National Bank Financial Group, Investors Group, Telus, the Baby Girl Project, Filmplan International II; FreeLife International, Friends of Iqbal; Gibson Foundation; Crofton House School; Sullivan Entertainment; DDB/Rapp Collins; Love Quotes; Lloyd A. Fry Foundation; Sudbury Minga for Maasai; Universal McCann; World Medical Relief; Nokia and Royal St. George's College.

Thank you to Marion Stewart, Joseph Koch, Jane Goodall, David Baum, Glen Kishi, Karen Radford, Jennifer Clarkson, Mark Caswell, Joan Brehl, Tim Broadhead, Patrick Johnston, Lis Travers, Donna Cansfield, Premier Dalton McGuinty, Rebecca Amyotte, Steve Miller, Sue Allan, Walter Green, Chris and Tania Carnegie, Terry Reeves, Judith Cunningham, Kate Dernocoeur, Liz Dowdeswell, Kathy Southern, Kerry Shapansky, Patricia Karen Gagic, Elaine Silver, Kim Phuc, Vito Maltese, Leo Ciccone, Dr. Mark Wise and Janelle McFarlane.

We cannot sufficiently sing the praises of the amazing team of staff and volunteers who are the soul of Free The Children and Me to We. The work of Free The Children and Me to We would not be possible without the dedication of many team members who work tirelessly on its mission. Free The Children is blessed to have the tremendous vision and leadership of Dalal Al-Waheidi, who has become family. Me to We's activities have been built by the unwavering dedication and hard work of Renee Hodginkson. Thank you to the leadership team of Victor Li, Janice Sousa, Erin Blanding, Lloyd Hanoman, Shobha Sharma, Peter Ruhiu, Michelle Hambly, William Qi, Erin Barton, Dan Kuzmicki, Lindsey Coulter, Sapna Goel, Allison Sandmeyer, Ashley Hilkewich, Scott Baker, Robin Wiszowaty, Marianne Woods, Kate Likely, Rann Sharma, Caeli Lynch, Alex Apostol and Louise Kent.

The efforts of our young members deserve special praise. Children and youth remain the heart and soul of Free The Children, and it is their dedication to building a better world that has allowed an after-school group to become the world's largest network of children helping children through education. Thank you to everyone who has decided to use their passion and gifts to make a difference!

Finally, our family deserves a heartfelt thank you, especially our Mimi, who remains our biggest fan. Finally, and most important, we wouldn't be where we are today without the love and support of our parents, Fred and Theresa. Thank you for everything, Mom and Dad!